To John Rodelli

The greatest challenge
we face as leaders is to
champion change and lead
people to a new level. I
admire your commitment to
growing your people at B of A.

Best wishes,

Jm Hinton
12.6.95

Customer-Focused
QUALITY

What to Do on Monday Morning

Tom Hinton / Wini Schaeffer

PRENTICE HALL
Englewood Cliffs, New Jersey 07632

Prentice-Hall International (UK) Limited, *London*
Prentice-Hall of Australia Pty. Limited, *Sydney*
Prentice-Hall Canada, Inc., *Toronto*
Prentice-Hall Hispanoamericana, S.A., *Mexico*
Prentice-Hall of India Private Limited, *New Delhi*
Prentice-Hall of Japan, Inc., *Tokyo*
Simon & Schuster Asia Pte. Ltd., *Singapore*
Editora Prentice-Hall do Brasil, Ltda., *Rio de Janeiro*

© 1994 by
Prentice Hall, Inc.

10 9 8 7 6 5 4 3 2 1

Library of Congress Cataloging-in-Publication Data
Hinton, Tom
   Customer-focused quality : what to do on Monday morning /
by Tom Hinton & Wini Schaeffer.
     p.   cm.
     ISBN 0-13-189630-X
   1. Customer service—Quality control. 2. Consumer satisfaction.
3.Total quality management. I. Schaeffer, Wini. II. Title.
HF5415.5.H55 1994   93-28070
658.8'12—dc20   CIP

ISBN 0-13-189630-X

PRENTICE HALL
Career and Personal Development
Englewood Cliffs, NJ 07632

Simon & Schuster, A Paramount Communications Company

Printed in the United States of America

For Megan, Rebecca, and Kelly

ACKNOWLEDGEMENTS

Because this book draws heavily on many years of business experience, it is impossible to thank everyone who has influenced this book. To them and even more importantly, to the many people who have assisted us directly on this book, we extend our sincere thanks.

During the time that we were working on the book, a number of people provided us with helpful suggestions and gave generously of their time. Although this list is too long to include, we would like to mention a few of these people.

As you, the reader, will learn, our friend Larry Dille was responsible for the subtitle; additionally, he and his colleague at Uarco, Steve Diller, helped keep us *focused* on our message. Richard Buetow of Motorola was another influence early in the process; his comments, after reading several of the initial chapters, were especially helpful.

Without the unshakable commitment to quality from the following people, there would be no book because it is their stories we have chosen to share with you. We are referring to Rob Davis at AT&T Universal Card Services; Janet Miller-Evans of Federal Express; Mary Alice Gonsalves and Joe da Rosa from Balboa Travel; Aleta Holub of The First National Bank of Chicago; Allan Juers with Towers Perrin; Martin Kaplan from Pacific Bell; Stephen King and Karen Stoeller of Harris Bank; Patrick Mene, The Ritz Carlton; Ron Norsell and Dave Klatt, Isuzu Truck of America; Joseph Harper, Craig Fravel and Julie Sarno, Del Mar Thoroughbred Club; and Phil Lee, The Leader's Edge.

Also, we want to acknowledge the special assistance and support of Karen Ehlert, Jean Hinton, and Marjorie Walden whose tireless efforts have helped to make this book a reality.

To **all** the many people who made this possible, thank you.

CONTENTS

PREFACE

When we began to write this book we believed then—and we are more convinced now—that quality is a "people" issue. This means that quality must be driven by senior management, include all of your employees, and, of course, address all of your customers in order to succeed. We believe that the most important reason a company should implement quality processes is to enhance its customer relationships, thereby achieving increased sales and profits.

Certainly, most businesses understand the importance of quality and its impact on customer satisfaction. Yet, throughout our discussions and research in writing this book, we realized that in many companies, something vital was missing. That "something," we discovered, was the link between *understanding* the importance of quality and *implementing* a customer-focused quality process. In short, we discovered that almost everybody believed in the quality gospel, but few were living it.

We began to ask questions such as, "Does your company have a quality process?" "If so, does it work?" "Do you listen to your employees and customers?" "How do you manage and measure your customer satisfaction and quality processes?"

It was at this point that we discovered an interesting—and even startling—fact. We learned that most businesses are *internally* oriented. In other words, they are still *company focused* not *customer focused*. Despite the wisdom of all the quality sages, the countless books and articles on this subject, and the thousands of speeches and conferences touting the importance of a commitment to quality excellence and customer service, too many companies are still missing the mark. Their culture is not customer focused, and not surprisingly, their results are often disappointing.

We think there are some valid reasons why companies, organizations, and governments are failing. And many of those reasons can be traced to three very basic factors:

1. Inattention to the customer
2. Inattention to the customer
3. Inattention to the customer

Customer-Focused Quality: What to Do on Monday Morning deals with how you go about paying attention to your customers by listening to, understanding, and meeting your employees' and customers' wants and needs. In many cases this process of understanding and responding will require significant cultural changes—changes that will be painful for some and easier for others. But these are changes that must be made in order for any business to be a viable global competitor.

Frankly, it takes guts to get started on a customer-focused quality process. It means destroying sacred cows in ritual fashion, stepping on toes, and working day and night to achieve results, and, perhaps, even risking a promotion. But the "quality choice" is one which we can control. We can still make a difference and affect the outcome—for the better! There are countless examples of North American companies and organizations that have used quality and a renewed commitment to their customers to not only save their businesses but, in fact, turn them around to become highly profitable.

A commitment to implementing a meaningful quality process that is truly customer focused can spell *success*. Success rarely comes from a lucky lottery card. We are convinced that it comes about from commitment, hard work, and leadership. But when success is achieved, many of the hardships are more than compensated for by the thrill of that achievement.

The subtitle of our book originated from a comment made by our good friend Larry Dille. Larry said that he had read a number of inspirational books on quality and that, while these books were motivating, they simply didn't tell him *how* to get started on a customer-focused quality process. They didn't tell him *what to do on Monday morning.* Larry has not only used some of this book, in draft form, as a guide for his company's quality program, but he has also provided us with some valuable insights on how he got started on Monday morning. We share many of his ideas with you.

In our book we have moved beyond the textbook theory and hoopla to provide you with practical "how-to's," coupled with the success stories of trailblazers and champions on their quests for quality. We offer this combination because we feel that the "how-to's" by themselves might be tedious or, possibly, not believable. The stories alone, as Larry pointed out, will not provide you, our readers, with insights on *how* to proceed. We have struck a balance that we hope provides you with both a readable book as well as a guide to helping your company achieve customer-focused quality.

In today's fast-paced, global environment, companies, government agencies, and nonprofit organizations have discovered that adopting a quality improvement process will increase their financial success, raise customer satisfaction levels, and create a reputation for excellence.

We hope you will accept the challenge to implement a meaningful, customer-focused quality process and, in so doing, give your business/organization a distinct edge in the competitive, global marketplace.

CHAPTER ONE

How to Champion Customer-Focused Quality

The journey of a thousand miles begins with a single step.

LAO TZU, Fifth Century B.C.
Chinese author of *Tao Te Ching*

Imagine being part of a dynamic and successful organization . . .

an organization that is committed to quality and strives for excellence in everything it does. . .

an organization that values its employees and its customers above all else. . .

an organization that accepts change as part of the natural evolution of its success. . .

What we imagine can become reality. Within the last few years, an increasing number of American companies have made this vision real. As we looked closely at these quality organizations, we began to realize that they have a lot in common. We reviewed, evaluated, and then distilled these best-in-class characteristics until we were able to convert our findings into ten vital action steps. These ten action steps for improving and maintaining quality provide the foundation for achieving customer-focused quality.

The ten steps are:

1. Make an irrevocable commitment to instituting a total customer-focused quality process in your organization.

2. Accept responsibility for championing your quality process.

3. Listen to your customers' requirements and measure their level of satisfaction on each of these requirements.

4. Develop a complete understanding of your employees' needs; communicate your vision and values and empower your employees to succeed.

5. Evaluate your processes and policies and benchmark them against the best-in-class.

6. Set goals for improving your practices, processes, and policies based on feedback from customers, employees, and best-in-class comparisons.

7. Establish a series of measurement systems to evaluate and track goal attainment and ongoing customer satisfaction.

8. Educate and train your employees in the ways of excellence.

9. Take delight in rewarding and recognizing the progress and achievements of your employees.

10. Begin anew; always seek to "raise the bar."

The best-in-class companies have honed the art of customer-focused quality. Recently recognized quality award winners like Federal Express, The Ritz-Carlton Hotels, and AT&T, for example, constantly recognize and reward their employees and monitor the level of service to their customers.

For all these organizations, striving to achieve customer-focused quality, it has meant a great amount of effort. For most, it was a long process, but for at least one company, the quest for excellence was achieved in fewer than three years. In December 1992, when AT&T Universal Card Services Corporation received the Malcolm Baldrige Award, the organization had been in businesss only two and a half years. In this short time, it had become the second largest company in the retail credit card business.

AT&T Universal Card Services ensures that it serves customers' and employees' requirements at every turn. It has established systems that learn about its customer needs *daily,* an effort that results in 4,000 customer calls a month. Processes are in place which constantly chart productivity and monitor improvement goals. We also especially like the fact that AT&T Universal Card Services employees constantly award each other for jobs well done. We've written more about this later in the book.

During the past three years, we have talked with people at AT&T Universal Card Services and dozens of other champions at companies which we believe are best-in-class in at least one aspect of their business. We will share many of these examples with you along with guidelines for implementing processes for quality improvement.

Not all of us, like AT&T Universal Card Services, can start with a clean slate. In many ways, longevity makes the introduction of quality processes harder. Unless a business entity is new or is very young at heart, there are significant hurdles to overcome, such as steel-like barriers of "We've always done it this way."

▼ HOW TO BEGIN

When you are trying to revitalize an established company, where do you begin? The first key is to make a *commitment* to being a champion for change and to convince others to be fellow champions. You and your colleagues must make an irrevocable commitment to raise your levels of quality and customer satisfaction. We believe this commitment is the first step toward achieving a *quality process.* Once you take that first step, it is unlikely that you will retreat.

This commitment, along with a keen and objective understanding of your customers, your employees, and your processes, is the initial key to achieving success and is prevalent throughout the institution of a quality process.

As you begin your quest for customer-focused quality, determine the level of support at the top of your organization. Clearly it is best when the CEO is strongly in favor of your efforts; be aware that at least some support will be required. If you are unable to gain this support, your efforts to establish a total quality process will be limited. You can relocate to another company or you can continue to make small indentations in improving quality, but changing the culture to a totally quality-focused organization is unlikely without support from the top.

We know of no way that is a guaranteed avenue to achieve CEO commitment to quality if an executive does not subscribe to its importance. It is sometimes possible to gain support through documentation of potential gains that could accrue through a total quality program. It may also be possible to gain support by referring to your vision and/or mission statement or creating one which, of course, will require CEO backing.

To review or create a vision or mission statement, you need to assemble a team that is representative of your organization. You may want to begin with a brainstorming session. Create an outline of the way you perceive your organization to be, and what you want it to be. Remember, at the outset of brainstorming, no idea is a "bad" one; cull later.

Another possibility is to start by reviewing the vision or mission statements of other companies and organizations. We have included several statements which we think are particularly good in Appendix 2 to this book.

As you discuss your ideas, list them. It sounds "low tech," but flip charts are helpful to use in recording ideas. During the process of recording, there are likely to be many rewrites. You may find that you'll want to return to prior statements, and, with a flip chart, unlike most marker boards, they'll still be there. Recording on a computer is great for note taking, but it does not allow the immediacy of a group's reaction to a thought.

Once you have a draft that has the team's approval, test it with a few appropriate people selected by the team, and then submit it to top management for changes or, in some cases, immediate approval. Then communicate your vision or mission to all; continue to communicate it on an ongoing basis through posters, cards, new employee training, and so on. Lastly, integrate all of your planning and processes with your vision and mission.

▼ QUALITY DOES PAY BACK

Championing a customer-focused quality program is hard work. The good news is that the results can be exhilarating. As you create quality processes, your people will react. Your customers will respond. Word will spread that doing business with your company is an exceptional experience. Customer retention rates will rise, profits will increase, and employee turnover will decrease.

A customer retention rate increase translates directly to profits. Since discussions about the effects of profit and/or cost savings can be transferrable to almost any business, the bottom-line impact of retaining profitable customers is a valuable sales tool in championing quality. Reichheld and Sasser in their *Harvard Business Review* article "Zero Defections: Quality Comes to Services," state that "Companies can boost profits by almost 100% by retaining only an additional 5% of their customers."

Reichheld and Sasser cite examples including MBNA, a Delaware-based credit card company. The president of MBNA assembled his employees and announced his determination that the company satisfy and keep all its customers. They gathered feedback on defecting customers and acted on the information to adjust and improve their processes. A plan was put in place which tied incentives to defection rates based on daily performance. The plan was structured so that for each day the company hits 95 percent of performance targets, MBNA contributes money to a bonus pool.

MBNA also introduced a customer-defection "swat" team staffed by some of the company's best telemarketers who determined why customers canceled their cards and attempted to persuade them to stay. This kind of action not only produces real-time information on where a firm needs to improve, but also helps reinstate customers. In MBNA's case, they were able to reinstate about 50 percent of the cancellers. As quality improvements were made, fewer customers left; MBNA's defection rate became one of the lowest in the industry and profits increased 16-fold. MBNA has found that a 5 percent improvement in defection rates increases its average customer value by more than 125 percent.

▼ YOUR ORGANIZATION IS UNIQUE

Once you have become a champion, the way may not always be clear. Nobody has traveled the same road you are about to travel. Although there will be paths which have been blazed by others who have traveled similar roads to quality, each company's journey has its own unique elements.

Fortunately, there are similarities as you travel the path to success—similarities about which we have written and which will help you get started. Ultimately, however, your company's quest for quality hinges on the level of your commitment to excellence and the effective implementation of improvements tailored to meet *your* customers' requirements.

In many ways, our book is a recipe—a mixture of techniques and carefully selected examples from best-in-class companies—for how to get close to your customers and take action on their suggestions and feedback to move forward in the quality process. It is important to note how closely the areas of success of these companies parallel the Malcolm Baldrige Award application guidelines; this holds true even among our examples of companies which have not received awards. Ours is a guide to use for designing and implementing a total process to improve customer satisfaction. Additionally, we encourage you to evaluate your company in terms of the Malcolm Baldrige guidelines even if you do not intend to be an applicant. To date, it continues to be the best benchmark we can find to measure your quality and customer satisfaction levels.

Certainly we hope to add some important "how-to's" to your quest for quality. Just as important, you will find that answers are often found in the heart and soul of a company—*its people*—as imbedded in the Ritz-Carlton staff discussed in Chapter 3.

There is not a single best-in-class company we know of that has not struggled to determine and implement quality processes. Every successful company has had to search for the answers just as you may be searching now. Constantly evaluate the answers of others in terms of how their solutions can apply to your company and then move forward.

America's great humorist Will Rogers once quipped, "Even if you are on the right track, you'll still get run over if you are standing still!" We hope to help you keep your company moving in the right direction so that your competition doesn't run past you even if you are on the right track! One only needs to compare the profitability of the *Fortune* 500 five years ago to that group today to understand and appreciate how the cost of poor quality, mediocre service, and a lack of empowerment can stifle a business and a nation.

▼ QUALITY IN AMERICA: THERE'S GOOD NEWS AND BAD NEWS

Quality in North America today is a "good news, bad news" story. On the one hand, the quality and service performance of many American businesses is improving because more companies are paying attention to their customers. It's that simple! But the bad news is that too many American companies are still not quality driven to the point where they can compete effectively with foreign companies around the world. What is at stake is the battle for economic superiority. The outcome of this battle will shape our nation's future for generations to come.

Fortunately, every company and organization has a secret weapon— its customers. Customers can help businesses win the quality fight because the solutions are there for the asking. Companies need to listen to their customers. They must make the commitment to sincerely listen, react, and then take that next critical step toward achieving the finest products and services possible based on their customers' needs and expectations.

If American businesses are going to compete—truly compete—on the basis of reputation, they must make a vigorous effort to regain their ranking as recognized leaders committed to producing quality goods and services. For this to happen, a greater number of people must become *champions of quality* for their organizations.

▼ GETTING "BUY-IN" OR CONCURRENCE

A portion of this book is devoted to quality and service champions—people who, in some cases, risked their jobs to help their companies become more profitable by challenging and, eventually, *changing the rules*—the old ways of doing things. These people are superb sales representatives because they have secured concurrence to move forward on quality improvements throughout their organizations.

These champions have called upon internal energy and courage they didn't know they had. Their stories cannot be fully told nor would they be directly transferrable from company to company. But, for those who are new to championship, we have found it is important to learn simply that others have faced a struggle and that many have succeeded in their pursuit of quality.

"Buy-in?" We've been asked repeatedly, "How do you get 'buy-in'?" that is, concurrence throughout an organization. It is clear to most of us who have worked within structured organizations that without "buy-in," change won't happen. We wish there was an easy formula to achieve this concurrence. But there is little that we have discovered. One unconventional process has yielded success stories. However, because it's multidimensional, that is, involving activity which is top-down, bottom-up, and whittling away at the middle, it is slow.

Some of you may have read about the little boy in England who was critically ill and whose wish was to be in the *Guiness Book of World Records* for receiving the greatest number of get-well cards ever. As a way to make the boy's wish come true, a chain letter was initiated.

The result almost overwhelmed the British postal system. The number of cards he received broke all records many times over and also gained him financial support for state-of-the-art medical care and the road to potential wellness. Even people who are wary of chain letters made calls and sent cards to this young boy. People can inspire and convince others to change or improve their lives. *A "chain reaction" can work.*

We don't suggest you begin with a chain letter per se, but consider an approach that creates the same effect. *Seek support at all levels, and ask people to convince others by showing them the benefits that can be accrued through change.* We call this a "terraced approach" to creating "buy-in."

When you look for your initial support, talk with as many people as possible; ask fellow employees whom you trust to help identify people who:

- Believe in the goal of driving a quality culture

- Are willing to risk working outside the system

- Can sell an idea or concept effectively

Since it is unlikely that others will be as zealous as you, or will have time allocated for this cause, you may need to help your supporters in their effort to convince others. *How do you help initiate change?* Consider the different personalities and leadership styles involved. Appeal to the broadest mix of people possible.

Four Ways to Initiate Change

1. You can provide your colleagues with an analysis showing potential cost savings and other benefits for the company and/or its departments by implementing the proposed changes.

2. You can share the successes of other companies or divisions of your company.

3. Through attending seminars and/or meetings of organizations such as the Conference Board or the American Society for Quality Control, you can determine the names of experts on quality improvement in the area you are championing and arrange for one or more of them to speak to groups in your organization.

4. You can give your supporters some of your time. This has a multifold benefit: not only do you help them, you get to know their operations better. Additionally, you get added "selling" time; this can really become a "win-win" situation.

As the change agents within your company gain greater conviction, they will begin to win over some of the people who have been sitting on the fence. Those converts, in turn, will convince others. Quite honestly, you are unlikely to receive 100 percent buy-in. But all you need is a majority at each level of your organization to succeed.

▼ CHAMPIONING

We believe that *champion* is the most important, unofficial title any employee can have in his or her organization. These people are the new breed of organizational heroes. Unfortunately, there have been times when they have also been the sacrificial lambs. But, happily, many quality champions have succeeded in converting others in their organizations into quality zealots. These champions and their converts have made an important difference in the quality of products and services in their companies.

Champion. . . the word has a positive ring because champion is usually defined as "a person who has defeated all opponents in competition and, thus, achieves first place." A secondary definition, "someone who fights for a person or cause," may be more appropriate here. But the primary definition does apply in that a champion frequently feels that it is necessary to "defeat all opponents in competition." Beyond that, it often seems that no one is cheering for his or her success.

Being a champion can be one of the world's most exhilarating experiences; it can also be one of the loneliest. Larry Zinski, Vice President and Director of Special Projects for Philip Morris, has a reputation as a *change agent* at his company. One of his successes was increasing market share by overhauling the sales process. Larry's efforts were focused on sales improvement rather than directly on quality, but the experience of championing is very similar. It is this experience that we wish to share with you.

Although today Larry can point with pride to a 4 percent increase in market share, which represents a significant sum of money, he still talks vividly about the loneliness of the championing experience. Larry told us about the financial costs, the roadblocks, and the period during which senior management became impatient. In fact, at one point,

Larry felt that his associates were reluctant to be seen with him, possibly thinking that Larry was courting potential failure.

When we evaluated what helped Larry succeed, we felt it was his conviction, his experience, and his thoroughly planned and well-executed strategy. Although it appeared to us that the strategy and efforts were largely Larry's, he did have the support of a consulting firm whose assurances to Larry's CEO that he was on the right track helped Larry gain the time and executive support he needed to do the job right.

An effort which is more directly related to quality improvement is one that is currently taking place at Pacific Bell.

Martin Kaplan, Executive Vice President of Pacific Bell, has been heavily involved in this improvement since 1984. The base of this change was a set of six commitments:

1. We are customer focused.
2. We value the individual.
3. We value communication.
4. We strive to be the best at what we do.
5. We value creative, can-do people.
6. We deliver the bottom line.

A total quality management system was put in place with the objective: "Be the Customer's Choice." The foundation and the components (as defined by the Malcolm Baldrige Award criteria, outlined in Appendix 1) of this system are shown in Figure 1-1 on page 14.

In talking with Marty, it became clear that he is a champion for superior customer service. He believes that Pacific Bell's competitive advantage is the company's best feature. The guidelines for this service are:

1. Be accessible when the customer wants to reach us.
2. Provide service through empowered professional customer advocates.
3. Deliver service when the customer wants it.

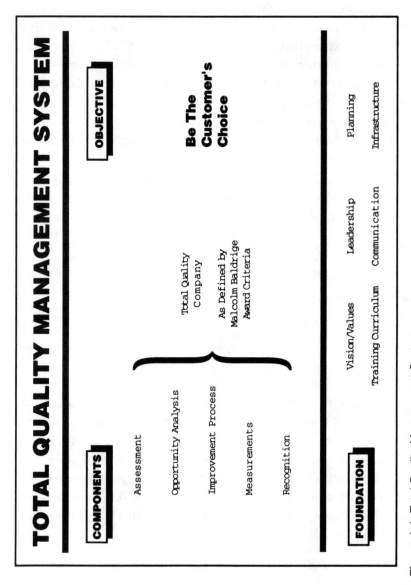

Figure 1-1 Total Quality Management System
Source: Pac Bell

14

4. Meet commitments.

5. Deliver service that works the first time, as promised.

6. Repair service problems before the customer is affected and correctly if the customer reports it.

7. Provide product support.

8. Assure flawless billing.

Change of the magnitude of Pacific Bell's, quite frankly, takes time. You can't give up. During his later years, Winston Churchill was asked to give the commencement address at Oxford. Churchill's commanding voice enveloped the crowd as he said, *"Never give up! Never, never, never give up!"* Saying only these few words, Winston Churchill walked from the stage. He had completed one of the most memorable speeches of all time and gave future generations a motto to live by.

Churchill's message is invaluable. We must stand by our convictions. *Change* means destroying "sacred cows." It means living through a period of being an *outsider*. Instituting a total quality program can be very difficult because in most cases you must first change the culture which drives the entire organization. As a consequence, it will require far-reaching commitments, including buy-in from senior executives and, *initially*, higher costs in time and resources.

But a quality-driven success will recoup those costs many times over, not only in terms of market share, but also in productivity and bottom-line dollars. Later, in Chapter 5, we talk about Motorola's goal setting for quality improvements. Through the significant product quality improvements Motorola has made over the past five years, this company estimates its current manufacturing cost savings at almost a billion dollars annually. Motorola predicts that the business process improvements, which are presently being put in place, will ultimately result in even higher cost savings.

Although it has been clear for some time that product quality is free, cost savings resulting from *service* improvements have not been as widely documented. Chicago Consulting found, based on work it did in both product-related and business process/service-related areas, that the savings from improvements in business processes are several times greater than those generated by product quality improvements. The First National Bank of Chicago, for example, has shown significant cost savings from improvements in business process productivity based on its cutting-edge quality efforts.

As a champion for customer-focused quality, you will be confronted with resource constraints, and you will need evidence that customer commitment positively affects profits. Examples of companies which have increased productivity, sales, and profits by increasing the quality of their products and services can be very useful.

Championing can also mean turning a business around by raising low morale and breathing quality back into the business. This requires someone who believes that people want to put forth their best effort and are capable of doing so.

In his book *A Better Idea*, Donald Petersen, the former CEO of Ford, talks about the revitalization of Lincoln-Mercury when it was at a low ebb in the midst of one of Ford's worst periods in the 1980s. Sales were down and morale was low. There was concern that if something was not done quickly, Ford risked losing a division that was a great source of potential profits. Gordon MacKenzie was asked to take a demotion to be the *champion* because he was viewed as the right man for the job. MacKenzie accepted the challenge in the true spirit of a *champion*.

As Petersen tells the story, "When Gordy moved over to Lincoln-Mercury, the place was in bad shape. An autocrat might have been extremely critical and relied on issuing orders. But Gordy was a team player whose approach was to say, 'You guys are the best. You just amaze me. You are fantastic.' He was such a cheerleader. Each step of the way, he brought the whole staff together. The environment quickly shifted from a negative to a positive one. Ben Lever, who had just returned from running Ford in Japan, was at Lincoln-Mercury when Gordy took charge and began to turn things around. To this day, Ben says it was one of the most exhilarating experiences he's ever had. If your company is trying to revitalize, what you need is a series of Gordy MacKenzies—a bunch of people who will go out there and get everybody excited about the challenges they face."

Gordy did not issue a series of commands or immediately change the way everything was done. What he did was rebuild morale; he changed the environment so that people automatically cared more about their jobs. When this happens, people, in turn, begin to initiate their own quality improvements. Much of Gordy's accomplishment stemmed from his people-oriented management style, a style which was apparently recognized when he was recruited for this tough assignment.

As a champion, each person brings her or his own style to the effort, but a positive, participative attitude can contribute significantly to success in creating constructive change.

▼ TAKING RISKS: BREAKING THE RULES

As a champion, you're going to break "rules." We are *not* suggesting doing anything which is unethical or illegal. *But we are advocating the need to change habit patterns, break familiar rhythms, and turn stones which "shouldn't" be turned.* These are patterns, rhythms, and anchors which have somehow evolved into "rules."

People have broken rules for years; most didn't "get caught." But this is a very different set of circumstances. *You have to get caught breaking the "rules."* You have to let people know that things can and should be done differently—that the "rules" need to change to enable quality and service success in your company.

We believe that, in many ways, empowerment began by people breaking the rules. Employees who were given the *responsibility* for serving the customer, but not the *authority* to help them, stretched beyond their job limitations and provided assistance beyond their spheres of authority. They sent out a replaceable part to get equipment running again or "OK'd" an overtime charge beyond their "job license." They "broke the rules."

When companies first begin to realize that policies are not adhered to, there is typically a reinforcement of those policies. On the other hand, when quality-driven organizations realize the positive effect of employees' going around established policies to give immediate assistance to customers, these policies are deleted or altered accordingly.

When one "breaks the rules," one can feel very alone. Most champions experience this. They perceive there must be a better way to achieve quality and customer satisfaction or that alterations are necessary for long-term survival. Other people in the organization may sense this as well. But they decide that it is safer politically to support the prevailing sentiment. Making change is fraught with risks. Most current champions—even past champions—cannot tell their entire stories because of potentially adverse political implications.

▼ WHAT IT TAKES TO BE A CHAMPION

A champion is the first to speak out—the first to take the risk. It takes *courage* to be a champion. When you begin to change the way things have been done for years, you need *confidence* that what you are doing is the right thing to do. When others say, "you're totally wrong"—and they will—you must have *conviction* to follow through. You must believe in your cause. You must be *committed*.

The network of relationships you have built through prior associations will be invaluable. These *connections* are likely to be the first source of help in building and promoting your case.

When decisions or actions are flawed, the champion is at greater risk of failure than usual because many people do not want champions to succeed. New ideas signal change and interrupt comfortable patterns. For this reason, champions must make decisions and act wisely. They need to ensure that they have the facts, understand potential consequences of their actions, and then pave the way. Champions must act with *prudence*.

Change is likely to take much more effort than imagined. Many times when you feel you have succeeded, an unforeseen roadblock appears. The champion's *perseverance* will be tested and retested.

Even the best ideas require salesmanship. A champion must make "the sale" over and over again. When some people have been convinced, there will still be others to "win over." Never-ending *persuasiveness* is critical.

Without a great deal of *patience*, there is little hope of overturning the many stones along the way. Championship takes time.

Characteristics of a Champion

- *Courage* to be a risk taker
- *Confidence* to speak out on behalf of the right thing to do
- *Conviction* to be relentless in "walking your talk"
- *Commitment* that what you are doing is the right thing to do—that it will make a difference
- *Connections* to help persuade, educate, and direct
- *Prudence* to make decisions thoughtfully
- *Perseverance* to retravel the same road often
- *Persuasiveness* to sell ideas at all levels
- *Patience* to continue until actions generate change

▼ MAKING CHANGE WITHOUT DESTROYING VALUE

We found that although change is vital to growth, some things do—and should—remain the same.

People's values, for example, rarely change. We want to be respected. We want to accomplish meaningful things in our life that make a difference. We want to be recognized for our accomplishments, and we want to be complimented for a job well done. This is true today. It was true yesterday, and it is likely to be true as long as people have feelings and are driven by a sense of accomplishment.

Few people understand *reactions to change* and continuity as well as Larry Dille, Vice President, Education/Standards of Excellence for Uarco, a manufacturer and supplier of business forms. When Larry talks about championing a quality program at Uarco, he first talks about people.

Despite Larry's long-standing comfort level with people and processes, when he was formally asked to assume the responsibility for managing Uarco's Commitment to Excellence program, at first, Larry couldn't decide where to begin.

We remember vividly his saying to us, "I've thought a lot about the importance of the commitment to excellence. I've read almost all of the books on quality. Some of these books have been very inspirational, but *"What should I do on Monday morning?"*

What Larry decided he should do on Monday morning was to think about Uarco's many people strengths and make sure his quality efforts continued to enhance them. He then began to review systematically all the quality processes that were in place at Uarco. *He identified not only where improvements needed to be made, but also determined which programs should **not** change.*

Often, there are a number of programs that should remain intact because they have enriched and are continuing to add value to the quality process. To quote Larry, "What would I have said to the employees as I dismantled our productivity improvement program—a program which has strong employee commitment and has reaped millions of dollars of savings for Uarco? Would I have told our people, 'We were only kidding about how important it was. . . we now have this totally new plan?' Would anyone buy into change under this scenario? It's not likely they would have." Because of the soundness of Larry's approach, we have included more specific information about quality processes at Uarco in Chapter 7, Leading by Example: Achieving a Reputation for Quality.

When we heard Larry talk about this, we thought, "Of course!" However, it has been our experience that people typically embark on a totally new, all-encompassing quality program without thoroughly examining their existing processes. By leaping before we look, one of the things which is usually missed is the identification of what should abide—what things should *not* change?

"I'm not trying to build a Quality Temple," Larry told us. But what Larry is doing is identifying, implementing, and improving a cohesive group of processes that will work or have worked for Uarco.

In talking with Larry, our thoughts about change and continuity were greatly clarified and magnified. We recognized the critical need to identify and hold onto those things which should stay the same— those things that effectively add value for our employees, our customers, and favorably impact the "bottom line."

Although we have discussed the importance of continuity and the need for keeping positive programs intact, this does not mean that we are less interested in our commitment to change. There is a place for both. Be sure that required changes continue to take place since it is easy for complacency to hide behind a mask of continuity.

Joel Barker, author of *The Future Edge,* talks in terms of paradigm shifts and changing the accepted model. We especially like his film on paradigms where he is riding a bicycle with a comfortable seat. It's much wider and more flexible than the traditional bicycle seat. "Bicycle seats were made to look like saddles," Barker says. Then he asks a probing question, "Why can't this be changed?" He goes on to explain that it's a model that bicycle manufacturers are reluctant to forfeit no matter how uncomfortable the seats are. While the shape of a horse and its saddle won't change, a bicycle seat *can* be changed.

▼ SUCCESS CAN BREED SUCCESS OR FAILURE

Many of our traditional ways of doing things are outmoded, uncomfortable, and restrictive. But we cling to our old ways because that's the way it's always been done. Most people are afraid of change. The *known* is preferred to the *unknown* until the discomfort level becomes too great or the new product is proven to be significantly better.

Those people who do welcome change and buy products in their embryonic stage are known as innovators or early adapters. Within the total market, very few people are early adapters. As companies move from serving these *early adapters* to gaining a larger segment of the population as their buyers, they become *growth* companies. The subsequent stage is *maturity*; the final stage is *aging*.

As companies reach maturity their leaders may take on a fear of change. After gaining the market's largest share, the leaders of these maturing companies cling to the formulas that created their business. Somehow they have forgotten that innovation was an important ingredient in their initial success.

Successful maturing firms are typically very profitable and have much to offer the economy. But these maturing firms often develop a monopolistic mentality. They become protective of their turf and waste a lot of money reinvesting in the old ways of doing business. They allocate their resources ineffectively and spend countless hours proving their way is *right* rather than exploring potential new products or developing service innovations.

Many become complacent and do not change until they face adversity. At that point it is too late for some because the competition will have surpassed them. Their success has bred impending failure.

But *success can breed success*. Those companies that use their resources to understand and react to marketplace change are the firms which continue to stay on top.

Making changes at a mature organization that doesn't have critical problems is difficult, but not impossible. Bob Nelson discusses this in his article, "Change Comes to the BBC," in the fall 1991 issue of *Forum Issues*. In 1988, Bob left British Airways, another "change success" company, to implement a major management intervention at the BBC. As he tells it, the BBC "appeared to be doing just fine. . . it enjoyed a stellar reputation . . . the BBC was a success story . . . why change?"

Although the BBC was "doing just fine," there were a number of changes taking place—political, financial, competitive, and technological changes that made management at BBC realize that they had to initiate a program of renewal if the BBC was to continue to be a communications giant.

Moving forward based on projected occurrences is critical in maintaining success. This is a very tough task. Nelson states that, "Asking people to change is a formidable challenge in and of itself; asking people to change from a perceived position of success can be very, very difficult."

After gathering an understanding of the culture, Nelson ran a series of week-long seminars for the organization's top 200 managers. Although he called it training, he states that it was really "leadership development intervention." His ultimate goal was to change the image of the BBC so that people would associate it not only with excellent programming, but with good management as well.

This program had what Nelson called a "rocky beginning." He states that "the training was not welcomed with open arms." But the work began to pay off about two years into the effort. This period of two years is important to note. *Change takes time.* The changes were an enhancement of communications, increased strategic thinking, and greater attention to needs identification and fulfillment.

Nelson concludes his article with a thought-provoking last paragraph:

> Perhaps the most important lesson I have learned is that change is a knife edge. If you push an organization too far, too fast, it might just bite you back. If you push it too cautiously, nothing happens. The trick is to get it just right. You never know if you have got it right until it bites back, or falls flat—and by then, of course, it is often too late. With the launch of a major change effort behind me, I can now say that the most exciting part of organizational development work is deciding when—and how—to take the plunge.

We recommend that you assess your culture and acknowledge the needs for change. Understanding your environment and your customers will help you identify these needs. Pay rigorous attention to what is going on around you and to your customers' requirements.

When a company listens to its customers and acts accordingly, it is likely to stay ahead of the competition. Ray Kroc at McDonald's enjoyed taunting his competition by urging them to steal his secrets for success because he would always be three days ahead of them with new and better ideas!

We look forward to the day when sincere concern for the customer will become foremost in all transactions rather than the unfortunate attitude that some people have developed that "serving customers takes too much time and keeps me from doing my work." Best-in-class companies recognize that "the customer *is* our work." Federal Express reminds its employees of this with each paycheck which states that a satisfied customer made this possible.

In summary

- Begin by making a commitment to customer-focused quality and becoming a champion for change.
- Review the vision and actions of companies that have successful quality processes and begin to adopt those philosophies and processes that best suit your company.
- Share best-in-class practices with your colleagues and show how quality improvements will benefit your firm.
- As you begin to institute change, be sure to leave valuable programs intact.
- Understand that championing means taking risks. You will need to "break the rules," that is, do things differently from the way they have been done before in your company.
- Move as quickly as possible in your pursuit of quality, but remember that change takes time.

CHAPTER TWO

How to Listen to Your Customers and Measure Their Satisfaction

We believe we see the world as it is. However, we really see the world as we are.

Understanding your customers . . . understanding your customers' requirements. Where to start? Start by asking your front-line employees who deal with your customers daily. Start by asking your customers. *Start by listening.*

We believe that *not* listening to customers has been the fundamental reason for business failure—the reason that companies have significantly lost strength or have gone out of business. The strong momentum of American industry in the 1960s and 1970s masked the surrounding threats to its sustenance. Change was so severely impeded by monopolistic mentalities that we are still suffering from the consequences. We became complacent; we listened to ourselves, not to our customers.

▼ THE CONSEQUENCES OF COMPLACENCY

In his excellent book on systems thinking, *The Fifth Discipline*, Peter Senge cites an example about a frog to illustrate how maladaptation to gradual business threats adversely affected the American automotive industry. We would like to carry his example a step further and suggest that through listening to and understanding your customers and then reacting to their needs, you can prevent "frog syndrome," which, you will note, can be fatal.

Senge writes,

> If you place a frog in a pot of boiling water, it will immediately try to scramble out. But if you place the frog in room temperature water, and don't scare him, he'll stay put. Now, if the pot sits on a heat source, and if you gradually turn up the temperature, something very interesting happens. As the temperature rises from 70 to 80 degrees F, the frog will do nothing. In fact, he will show every sign of enjoying himself. As the temperature gradually increases, the frog will become groggier and groggier, until he is unable to climb out of the pot. Though there is nothing restraining him, the frog will sit there and boil. Why? Because the frog's internal apparatus for sensing threats to survival is geared to sudden changes in his environment, not to slow, gradual changes.

Unless we constantly monitor our performance and sincerely listen to the voices of our customers, we become complacent. Just as the higher water temperature wasn't apparent to the frog until it was too late, the impact on market share usually doesn't become evident until it's too late to make the necessary changes to save the bottom line. Unless a firm has other highly profitable areas or a stash of cash, when a pivotal part of the organization becomes complacent, it, like the frog, may not survive.

Understanding your customers' expectations and making the appropriate changes to improve customer satisfaction is possible only if you first *listen* to what your customers say and then move quickly to act upon their suggestions. Listen as if you were an *objective outsider*. Sometimes this is difficult to put into practice. Why?

For one reason, our biases get in the way, superimposing themselves on the words and feedback we hear. Before the customer has finished his or her thought, we're already making a judgment and formulating our response. It's human nature, but nevertheless, it disrupts our listening.

Many of us have become lazy listeners. An example of this, which is even better when verbalized, was given at a seminar on listening that we attended.

Q. What do you call a tree that has acorns?
A. Oak.
Q. What do we call a funny story?
A. Joke.
Q. What do we call the sound made by a frog?
A. Croak.
Q. What do you call the white of an egg?

Think twice or you may respond *yolk* because we sometimes respond according to traditional rhythms or create mental pictures with preconceived answers. But the white of an egg is, of course, an *egg white* or *the white of an egg.*

Additional explanations for tendencies to respond yolk are that we listen in spurts or that we hear sounds and words, but only half-listen. Listening can be categorized in three ways.

Level 1. Listening in Spurts. When listening in spurts, we tune in and tune out to what the speaker is saying. Although we're aware of the other's presence, *we are thinking of what we want to say.* When we listen in spurts, we may miss the intent of the message; we are primarily paying attention to ourselves not to others.

Level 2. Hearing Sounds and Words, but Only Half-listening. At this level, we hear the sounds and words, but *we miss the intent* of the speaker's message. We hear the cadence but miss the meaning.

Level 3. Active Listening. At this level, people refrain from evaluating the speaker's words and put themselves in the other person's position. Active listeners devote full attention to the speaker capturing the idea and reserving judgment. The one characteristic that distinguishes active listeners from the other styles is that they always *listen for the* intent and *meaning of the message.*

Stop, look, and *listen actively* to your customers. They possess invaluable golden nuggets collected from many business transactions with you. They know your strengths and weaknesses. They can tell you in a heartbeat what works and what doesn't—and why! But they rarely volunteer this information or let you explore this gold mine of customer data unless you *ask* them.

Listen for your customers' requirements. What are their expectations of your company and what do they want from you by way of service and quality? Be careful not to hear what you *believe* to be their requirements. Sometimes a customer may think that she has a good solution, and you may believe that your solution is a better one. In fact, your solution may indeed be better, but if your customer doesn't think so, it really doesn't matter.

If you truly understand your customer's needs, you can talk convincingly about *why* your way is better. But, be careful that you don't irritate the customer in the process. Another tack you might take is to tailor your solution to fit the customer's wishes. Be flexible and open to new ways of solving customer problems.

Why change your position to suit your customer? The answer boils down to dollars and "sense." If you don't remain flexible, it's likely that your competitors will. And, if you encourage your customer to experience the competition for all the *wrong* reasons, you just might lose the sale and, possibly, that customer for life!

▼ LISTENING TO CUSTOMER COMPLAINTS

One of the questions we're often asked is: "How do you track complaints?" The inquirers are then likely to add, "We want to really understand what our customers think of us." Since only 4 percent of your customers are likely to complain, be careful! The complaints of that 4 percent may be different, and possibly of lesser importance, than the complaints of those who did not let you know that they were unhappy but moved on to do business with your competitors.

A complaint tracking system is a valid measure of how your customers feel about you only if you determine that there is a strong positive correlation with customer satisfaction measurement survey results—survey results which include a representative sample of current and *former* customers. Cluster your complaints by their cause; see if there is a recurring pattern indicating a process which may need to be improved. Otherwise, devote your time to tracking customer loyalty, developing an objective customer satisfaction measurement process, and ensuring that you listen to and handle complaints effectively.

Here's a five-step strategy we recommend for listening and handling complaints:

1. Acknowledge the customer in a sincere way even though the customer might be less than pleasant due to his or her negative experience.

2. Listen patiently and without interruption as the customer tells you his or her experience. Offer empathy and understanding. If you need more information, simply inject the phrases, "Then what happened" or "How did that make you feel?"

3. Restore trust by aligning with the customer so he or she knows "you are on his or her side." Under these difficult circumstances, a customer may view you as the enemy. Reassure the customer that you want to help solve the problem.

4. Indicate ways in which you intend to resolve the problem. If you are unable to determine a solution, and if it is appropriate, ask the customer for suggestions.

5. Follow up. We're amazed that so many companies never follow up with a customer to see if everything is okay. This is your company's chance to not only regain a dissatisfied customer, but win his or her loyalty for life.

Sometimes, when you listen to your customers' perceptions, you may think the customer is *wrong*. Although a customer may not be technically correct, you should remember that it may have been your company that created the customer's perception in the first place by something it did or failed to do. It is up to all of us to probe customer perceptions and our quality/service processes to find the clues. Don't reject perceptions because they seem invalid. Somewhere, there is likely to be a grain of truth. Most important, it is *your customer's* perception. That's how they see you—for better or worse, that's their reality! The customer may not always be right, but the customer should always feel he or she won.

▼ LISTENING AS A BUILDING BLOCK
TO SUCCESS

Listening is an essential building block to achieving service and quality success. Throughout our interviews, listening to their customers was one of the practices which every best-in-class company identified as crucial to their quality service process.

▼ CADILLAC'S THREE-STEP APPROACH
TO CUSTOMER SATISFACTION

For example, to create true customer satisfaction, the Cadillac Motor Car Division of General Motors, a 1991 Malcolm Baldrige Award winner, committed to studying the ownership experience from cradle to grave. In order to ensure customer satisfaction, Cadillac developed a three-step process which began with listening to its customers. First, Cadillac asked its customers what they needed and expected in a luxury car. Based on these findings, Cadillac translated these customer needs and expectations into world-class products and services. To ensure continued service and build long-term customer relationships, Cadillac then instituted an "after-purchase" support program.

Cadillac uses extensive market research to collect customer feedback and service information. Future products and features are tested extensively in vehicle clinics where potential customers rate them against current models from the competition. This feedback helps Cadillac's Simultaneous Engineering Teams to focus on the customer and build a better car. Cadillac also conducts "after-purchase" research to gauge vehicle performance, assess customer satisfaction, and size up the target market. The loop is completed by sharing this valuable data with Cadillac's 1,600 dealers.

We've noticed a few important things about people who are known to be, or trained to be, good listeners. Trained listeners:

- Listen completely before responding.
- Defer judgment.
- Are more controlled.
- Listen closely for content.
- Try to understand nuances of meaning.
- Try to determine the other person's feelings.
- Rarely "get hung up" on appearances or form.
- Concentrate on major ideas.
- Stay focused on the main issue.

Dr. Lyman Steil of The Sperry Corporation developed ten keys for effective listening that we present in Table 2-1. His "effective listener" echoes our observation of the trained listener— the lack of judgment until comprehension is complete, the avoidance of distractions or becoming sidetracked, and the listening for central themes.

Table 2-1 Ten Keys for Effective Listener

Listening Keys	The Poor Listener	The Effective Listener
1. Find areas of mutual interest.	Tunes out dry subjects.	Seizes opportunities; asks "What's in it for me?"
2. Judge the content, not the delivery.	Tunes out if delivery is poor.	Judges content, skips over delivery errors.
3. Hold your fire.	Tends to enter into an argument.	Doesn't judge until comprehension is complete.
4. Listen for key ideas.	Listens for facts.	Listens for central themes.
5. Be flexible.	Takes intensive notes using only one system.	Takes fewer notes; uses four or five systems.
6. Work at listening.	Shows no energy output; fakes attention.	Works hard, exhibits active body state.
7. Resist distractions.	Is easily distracted.	Fights or avoids distractions, tolerates bad habits, knows how to concentrate.
8. Exercise your mind.	Resists difficult material; seeks light, recreational material.	Uses heavier material as exercise for the mind.
9. Keep an open mind.	Reacts to emotional words.	Interprets color words; does not get hung up on them.
10. Your rate of thinking is faster than speech.	Tends to daydream with slow speakers.	Challenges, anticipates, mentally summarizes, weighs the evidence, listens between the lines to tone of voice.

Source: Dr. Lyman Steil, The Sperry Corporation.

Think more about how you listen. Then in your next discussions with customers and employees, you may find yourself listening differently. Listen to what your customers and your employees have to say. Be sure you understand their language, their concerns, and their requirements. Then, respond by taking actions to serve their needs to every extent possible.

Listen to Your Front-Line Employees

Before you talk with your customers about their requirements, we suggest that you talk with your front-line employees—those people who interface with your customers daily—in sales, service, and especially in the area of customer support. They are the people who are most likely to know how your customers feel about your firm. They are also the most likely to speak your customers' jargon. Ask them a series of questions such as:

- What are the compliments most frequently paid to our company?
- What do you think our customers like best about doing business with our firm?
- Where and when do misunderstandings with customers most frequently occur?
- What customer problems do you encounter most frequently?
- What processes should be corrected to benefit the customer?
- Where do you, the employee, feel you lack the authority to help the customer? What is your recommendation?

It's amazing what you will learn from this internal assessment. It will provide you with the keys to customer priorities and even more important, keys to improving your level of service to your valued customers.

Pay Attention to Your Successes

Notice that we started our employee questions with inquiries about the positive aspects, the satisfactory perspective. When we think about and talk about customer satisfaction measurement, too often we really mean customer *dissatisfaction*. We closely analyze the things we do *wrong* and take actions toward improvement. Although we are happy about the good ratings, we rarely analyze them or understand how important they are to our customers. The net result of not understanding customer satisfaction is that we could eliminate something we do especially well, thus forfeiting a factor that makes us a preferred supplier without realizing it. At best, this creates additional effort. At worst, it means lost customers.

Be sure you understand customer **satisfaction** *as well as dissatisfaction. Pay at least as much attention to your* **successes** *as your failures.* Your successes may be the key to your continued competitive edge.

Listen to Your Customers

After you've talked with front-line employees, you must talk with your customers. If you talk with customers frequently, you have an advantage, but you may also have biases. Are you talking with a representative sample of your customers or only those with whom you are comfortable? Has your focus been on *their needs*? Often customer discussions revolve around a particular issue. Important? Very! But this is unlikely to enhance your understanding of your customers' *overall* requirements.

Talk to your customers about their business and listen to how you can best serve them. Ask them to talk about one of the last experiences they had in doing business with you and what was good and bad about that experience.

▼ DETERMINING WHO YOUR CUSTOMERS ARE

Who is your customer? This question sounds simple, but it's not! *Don't even think of beginning the assessment process until you are sure you know who should be interviewed.*

It is amazing how a group of people in the same department will initially disagree when asked, "Who are your customers?" Some will identify the customer as the purchaser; others may say it's the decision maker, or the installer, or the ongoing user. In some instances, these could all be the same person functioning in different roles. But these could also be four different people. If, at a particular firm, it is four different people, you may need to talk with all four to get a complete picture of how that firm views doing business with your company. In business-to-business situations, it is frequently the case that more than one person influences the purchase decision.

Typically, business-to-business surveys are conducted based on names in the company files. These names are frequently the names of the purchasing agent. Yet, this purchaser—the person who is most frequently questioned in research—may have only cursory awareness of the decision process or the after-sale product or service performance. It is very important to determine upfront who your customers are and ensure that those with whom you talk are representative of all the people who interact with your company.

If you sell through distributors, it is important that both the distributor and the end users of your product are included in the research.

Having more than one type of customer extends beyond the corporate environment. In a study for a university, for example, the appropriate respondents may include students, faculty, administrative personnel, trustees, and/or parents of students, depending on the research requirements. Similarly, in a hospital, the appropriate respondents could be former patients, medical staff, administrative staff, board members, benefactors, and so on, depending, again, on the research requirements.

▼ THE IMPORTANCE OF SETTING OBJECTIVES

Prior to your customer meetings, work with your colleagues to determine your overall objectives. These objectives may be based on information from other studies you have done, priorities in your organization, goals, or strategic plans. But *the key objective of this first phase should be to provide insights of what your customers expect from you.* Remember that this phase is an overview to assist you in understanding the factors which are important to your customers. These factors are the ones you will want to measure in your customer satisfaction research. A thorough customer satisfaction survey process is multi-stepped and, quite honestly, takes considerable time.

More often than not, when customer interview data are requested, information is wanted "yesterday" and people want a large "statistically significant" sample. To respond to this urgent need for data, a questionnaire, which is often more aligned with internal points of view than with customers' perspectives, is written and sent to a large number of customers.

Results of this kind of research are significant only about the questions someone thought to ask and represent only the views of those people who sent them back. Were the questionnaires sent to the appropriate people? What about the questions the customer wished you had asked? What about those important people who didn't respond?

Even if the questionnaires were sent to the people who were best suited to answer the questions, those recipients who were *really* dissatisfied with your company or service are likely to toss the questionnaire in the wastebasket.

Recently a colleague came into our office and said, "You're interested in customer satisfaction, what do I do with this?" It was a questionnaire regarding service on her car. Her answers to all the questions were positive; her car appeared to be expertly fixed and the service was timely. But getting an appointment was a "nightmare." The dealer/service establishment hadn't included a single question about its telephone system or their service schedulers, and there was no space for write-in comments. Our colleague never intends to return to that dealer, but the dealer is unaware of losing her as a customer.

No research is better than poorly designed or poorly executed research. With no research you act on your own best judgment. With inept research, you may have a strong, potentially inaccurate feeling that you are really good and may not find until the end of the year that you have lost business.

With poorly designed or poorly executed research, you may not know the importance of those things you are doing right or be aware of your most serious flaws. You need to build on the things you do right; don't neglect them or eliminate them. You also need to know what to "fix first."

Really dissatisfied customers may have thrown the questionnaire in the wastebasket; mildly disgruntled ones are more likely to answer. Their problems should be fixed, but what is the appropriate level of priority for this? If you have inadequate research, you may not know the problems encountered by your *former* customers or those who are *most* dissatisfied with your products or services.

It is critical that you have a thorough understanding of your former customers and those customers who are really dissatisfied. If they left because of problems with your company, these problems, if unresolved, should be your highest priority because others are likely to leave for the same reasons. Normally, it is best to use a third party to contact former customers. However, we have heard of suppliers regaining customers by taking the time to visit former customers, listening objectively, and then working through the issue that caused them to leave.

Without a proper identification of your customers, agreed-upon objectives, and thorough qualitative research upfront, it is unlikely that the results of customer satisfaction research will yield a significant reading of what you really need to know. *If you don't ask the right questions of the right people in the right way, you are wasting your money!*

This wasted money is not just research dollars. When you receive negative responses from those who respond, it is likely that you will spend a lot of money fixing those problems. Admirable? In some ways, yes. But remember that your resources should be directed toward correcting your *major* sources of dissatisfaction *first*. You need thorough research to identify and isolate your most critical problems and determine those which will impact your market share.

▼ PREPARING A DISCUSSION GUIDE

When you have determined your objectives, prepare a discussion guide. We are not talking about a questionnaire at this stage; in fact, this guide is often called a topic outline. Most of the topics should not be in structured question format because you should allow the conversation with your customers to flow. The outline serves as an important reminder to keep your focus on *satisfaction criteria* and the areas of interest which you have designated.

When you develop the outline, you'll want to refer back to your objectives and include subjects that are most important to your firm as well as areas where other customer contact has indicated you may be performing especially well—or where you feel that you may not be living up to your customers' expectations. But remember you are trying to determine, first and foremost, what your customers consider important in their business transactions with you.

People who are embarking on customer satisfaction surveys invariably ask us to send a questionnaire or give us examples of our research findings. We always say "no." The reason for our response extends beyond the proprietary nature of customer satisfaction research. We believe that *your* questionnaire should be based on what *your* customers think is important in doing business with you. Each business is different. One size does not fit all. You must ask your customers the factors which are important to them.

Initial informal, personal interviews will provide you with this information—the information which will provide the framework for your questionnaire. To enable you to start this process, we will provide you with some important areas to include in your topic outline and some suggested questions to use at the outset of your discussion. Some questions we recommend asking are the following:

- What do you like best about doing business with (or dealing with) us? How important is this factor to you in terms of our relationship with you?

- What do you like least about doing business with (or dealing with) us? How important is this factor to you in terms of our relationship with you?

- What one thing could we do to significantly improve the product or service we provide to you?

- What one thing could we do to improve our customer service?

- What are the most important factors in doing business with us? (You can request a number or numbers here such as the six or eight most important.)

- Do you recommend our firm to others?

Remember to keep your objective in mind; think of the information you need upon completion of your interviews. Subjects which are generally important to cover are:

- *The respondent's responsibility* and his or her interface to your firm and the *names of others you should talk to.*

- *The last interaction* the respondent had with your firm and *the results* of that exchange.

- The respondent company's *buying decision process.*

- An *overall opinion* of each of your products/services about which he or she is knowledgeable.

- An understanding of *important factors in* individual *functional areas* (e.g., sales/service response and knowledge, delivery, and invoicing) and the degree to which they are important.

- *Expectation levels and definitions of excellence* in each functional area, for example, what is meant by "on-time delivery?" (In a manufacturing environment, where a "just-in-time" process is practiced, *early* is not a satisfactory option; similarly, for a gourmet restaurant, *fast* can be faulty unless, perhaps, you're located in the theater district.)

A more explicit example of the kinds of things you learn that are unexpected, the important "Aha's," as we call them, may be appropriate here. Unless you ask the customer his or her definitions of terms such as "on-time" delivery, you may be missing important causes of why your customers may be dissatisfied with you. We know of one company, which when they went through this process, encountered a big surprise. When a customer said to them that they had a serious delivery problem, the supplier company said, "That can't be; we know we're not perfect, but we measure our on-time deliveries and 96 percent of the products we send to you are delivered on time." The customer then said, "Yes, this is true, but you are measuring by product; we measure by completeness of an order. I need 100 percent of my order of your products before I can begin assembly of my product. Therefore, any delivery which does not include 100 percent of my order may as well be no delivery."

If this supplier had not conducted preliminary interviews and had written a questionnaire on customer satisfaction to send to their customers, they may not have even included a question on delivery; after all, they had a measurement system and thought they knew their performance. Assuming that the supplier had included a question on delivery, the answer would have appeared to them to be wrong because it is very unlikely that they would have known why the customer was dissatisfied.

Understanding your customer's point of view is there for the asking, but few of us ask!

We don't ask because we're too busy, because it's too time consuming, or too expensive, or worse, because we think we know. Short term, it often does not matter, but over the long term, a competitor may take our place if we don't invest in learning as much as we can. *Knowledge is power, and utilizing information can reap profits.*

▼ SCHEDULING AND CONDUCTING CUSTOMER INTERVIEWS

We believe that the first phase of a customer satisfaction research process should be to conduct personal interviews. When you arrange these, understand that you may need to schedule them weeks in advance. You should allow at least an hour for a discussion with one person, and at least an hour and a half for a discussion with more than one person. Your salespeople should be alerted and can help make the initial contact but should not be present at the interview. Their familiarity with the account may impact the objectivity of the interview.

Obtaining the information you require can be accomplished by talking with one person at a time or through discussions with people who represent different functions within the same customer company. For example, these could be representatives from Purchasing, Accounting, Service, and/or Systems. These are people who typically do not talk with each other on a day-to-day basis. They may, in fact, have never met. Yet each may in a different way, influence the selection of your product or service.

Often when a situation is created that allows people across functions to interact, they realize that this is beneficial to them as well as to your research. It often creates rich dialogue and cooperation which provide a complete profile and unique insights into doing business with your company.

The downside of holding group discussions is that they can be inhibited by consciousness of job levels, particularly outside the United States. They also may take additional time to schedule. One-on-one interviews are a preferred alternative in many situations, but each of the critical functional people should be interviewed.

▼ ASSIMILATING AND EVALUATING DATA

The next step is to assimilate and evaluate all the information obtained from your employees and your customers. The major things which you are looking for here are

- Factors that are most important to your customers.

- Areas where your customers feel you excel or disappoint.

- Clues to how your market may be segmented that may differ from your traditional segmentation.

- Relationships between what your front-line employees and customers have told you.

You should now have a more objective understanding of your business and a good base for proceeding. At this point, we suggest that you hire an external consultant or market research firm.

The primary reason that we feel this is important is objectivity. The secondary reason is that working with an external firm will provide you with competitive data comparable to your own. Additionally, customer satisfaction research is becoming more of a science. Complex trade-off techniques for buyer behavior as well as computer programs which enable sophisticated analysis are constantly being refined. A good research firm will provide this, which will greatly enhance the value of interview output and results.

If budgets or other factors preclude hiring an outside firm, then work with a person or persons who have expertise in sample design and questionnaire writing to help you take what you have learned to date and develop a more structured interview process based on that information. Within your company, these skills should certainly reside in a market research department, but can also often be found in the human resource or training areas. Statistical expertise can be found in engineering or other technical areas as well.

Although we strongly prefer the use of an outside firm at this stage of the research, there are some advantages to using your own people. If you are conducting thousands of interviews, some interviews may have to be done by your employees for cost reasons. "In-house" interviewing can also enable you to identify and respond immediately to customer problems.

▼ HOW TO IDENTIFY CUSTOMER SATISFACTION RESEARCH FIRMS THAT CAN MEET YOUR NEEDS

The best way to identify market research firms or consulting firms which are skilled in customer satisfaction research is to ask other companies who they have used, whether the results have resulted in increased market share for their company, and whether they have had a good working experience with that firm.

Once you have the names of several firms, ask them to come to your location and talk about their firm and their methodology. Tell them about your firm, how your customer base is structured, and a little of what you have learned from your initial interviews. At this point you will know which two or possibly three firms are most likely to meet your requirements. Ask these firms to submit a proposal on how they would structure the survey, who would work on the project, and what the cost of each phase would be.

▼ WORKING WITH AN EXTERNAL RESEARCH FIRM

Best-in-class consultants or market research firms will want to understand what you have learned from your employee and customer discussions, but they should also repeat much of the process. They, too, will begin by talking to your employees and then talking to your customers as well as potential customers, lost customers, and competitors. You may think this step is redundant, but based on our experience, it is clearly value added.

The consulting/research firm which you have selected should have discussions with members of your management team whose functions are directly customer related. Through these discussions, you enhance the consultants' understanding of your company, and you also provide management with an upfront understanding of the objectives of the research. This is especially important because the functional management people in your firm will be responsible for acting on the research findings.

It is essential that you spend sufficient time with the research firm. You'll want to have in-depth discussions not only about your customer and employee discussion findings, but also about your business, your marketplace, and what you know about your competition. Also, talk about other quality measures in your company and the potential linkages that your planned research should have with that data.

Throughout the process, you need to work with the research firm and ensure that they are meeting your objectives and that they are letting you know about problems that may emerge with your customers that need to be resolved immediately. Do not just hand the project over until time for them to issue a report; view this as a joint venture to help improve your customer satisfaction.

▼ SEGMENTING YOUR MARKET

Whether you hire a consulting firm or do the research yourselves, market segmentation is important to the success of your survey research. Think about your marketplace and your customers and how they are normally segmented. Typically, you will find that there are two different kinds of segmentation. The first is easier to categorize; known as demographic, it includes designations such as geographic trading areas, industry types, company size, family size, and so on. The second is behavioral and is based on function or experience: a technically oriented buyer may be different from a creative one or a financially oriented one, and so on. When a sample is designed, it is important to attempt to predesignate these segments so that you will have adequate data in each.

Included in this segmentation is the fact that distributors and dealers need to be separated from end users. In many cases, it is also important to interview your distributors' customers. Through promising the distributors the data, particularly if you are working with a third party where names can remain anonymous, this is feasible.

▼ DEVELOPING THE QUESTIONNAIRE AND SAMPLE

The advantage of having background about your customer and your marketplace before you begin the quantifiable stage is that the questionnaire and sample design become almost self-evident. We have paid attention to segmentation which is critical in sample selection, plus we now know the factors that customers consider to be important. These are the factors we will use when we ask our customers about their level of satisfaction in dealing with us.

We also know customers' definitions of factors, so that our structured interviews can be concise and take less interview time. Because the structured interview process may be administered by telephone, this precision is particularly valuable.

Although you should work out the sample, the methodology, and the questionnaire with a market research firm or people in your company who are skilled in these areas, we want to share some of our experiences in this regard. These are based on results which have been most useful for us and, in the long run, have saved money.

Oversample Key Accounts and Potential Key Accounts

When we have employed a "pure" random sample, we have felt cheated because we knew that a large share of our dollars came from a relatively small number of accounts and only a few of those were included in the data. Oversampling of large accounts will correct this. However, you need to be aware of taking excessive amounts of your customers' time to answer questions. *Don't "overinterview" key accounts.*

Also, remember that if your company is identified as the sponsor of the research, these important customers will expect immediate reaction to their concerns. A consultant or market research firm can shade your identity and give you more time to address these concerns. However, you need to weigh this against the benefits for your firm in being identified as the interview sponsor. Customers are often very positive about the fact that you are spending money to get their opinion. We have also found that potential respondents are more willing to participate in a survey when the sponsor firm is identified.

Conduct Prescheduled Telephone Interviews

We generally prefer telephone over mail surveys for ongoing business-to-business surveys. When we include the telephone follow-up which is required to verify that the mail survey returns are statistically representative of the customer population, we have found that costs of mail surveys are similar in cost to telephone surveys. Surveys conducted by telephone also help ensure that the appropriate persons are responding and enables dialogue which enriches your data. If a survey is especially complex, a combination of telephone and mail is appropriate.

Although we almost always favor *in-person interviews,* personal interviews are generally too costly at this stage of the research due to the number of interviews required. How many interviews? There is no magic number. A sample which is significant can be designed only after you have determined how you want to segment the data, that is, in how many different ways you want to look at the results. Do you want to understand the information by region? By industry? By size of customer? Within each of these, how many categories exist?

Use a Numerical Scale with a Midpoint

Up to this phase of the data gathering process, you have had a lot of opportunity for open-ended dialogue. Although this can and should continue, you should now use structured questions. Some of these should require answers on a numerical scale. This is critical because this becomes your baseline for understanding customers' expectations, goal setting, and trend analysis.

In instances where a scale is employed, we usually prefer a scale with a midpoint. (An example of a midpoint is a "3" on a scale of 1 to 5). Why a midpoint? This means neither satisfied nor dissatisfied, neither happy nor unhappy; it means your customer may stay or leave. Without the midpoint, you force an answer which is "like" or "dislike," when, in fact, the customer may be neutral. This means that you have a good chance of keeping that customer if you try a little harder. At the same time, you also stand a good chance of losing that customer to your competitor if you don't improve.

It is also important to define the anchors of the scale, that is, designate *all* points on the scale in words to help ensure the respondents have a consistent understanding of the scale's value. (Examples of anchors are "5" is very satisfied; "1" is very dissatisfied.)

Allow the Respondent to Say Easily He or She Doesn't Know

We don't want answers when a person has had insufficient experience with a particular aspect of our product or service. Not providing for a "don't know" and/or "not applicable" response forces false answers in many cases; these answers can skew the results. "Don't knows" can be valuable. In some cases, a respondent may have no reason to know. In others, it can tell you that you may need to educate some of your customers about a particular product or aspect of your service.

Develop a Ranking of Important Factors

It is critical now that you have asked customers to identify what is important to ask *how important* these factors are vis-à-vis each other. It is only then that you know what to fix first when problems emerge and, conversely, what is especially important to continue doing well.

If you work with a market research firm, they may use conjoint analysis (a form of trade-offs using paired comparisons) or another analytical technique to accomplish a ranking of the factors. We believe that this is the optimum way to accomplish ranking of factors. Simpler ways are to ask customers to rate the importance of each factor or the factors in order of importance to them. Since customers have already identified these factors as important, the discrimination among them can be difficult. However, this step is one which should be included.

It is a safe bet to guess that your resources are limited. This means that it is unlikely that you will have the people, power, or the funds to correct all your problems immediately. We have seen some relatively good survey results that didn't lead to improved customer satisfaction because those responsible for making changes tried to improve everything at once. Due to resource constraints, everything got improved a little, but not enough for customers to sense the difference.

Because the research identified the problems, but did not give relative importance to their weight, there was a weak attempt to fix all. As a result, problems number one and two remained problems number one and two, and customers remained dissatisfied. It is at this point that *your* competition can call on *your* customers and gain a piece of *your* market share. The major sources of your customer dissatisfaction can be resolved more readily if you focus your efforts on the key problems first, not diffusing your efforts. Let your customers know as soon as possible that you are listening and that you have incorporated their suggested changes to serve them better.

Share Results with your Customers

With satisfaction research, sharing results with your customers isn't as straightforward as it may be with some other types of research, where we often advocate sharing. By sharing customer satisfaction results, others can easily learn your strengths and weaknesses. When your firm is not identified in conjunction with the research, you can easily remain anonymous. (When you use an external firm to conduct the research, the choice about whether to identify your company as the research sponsor is usually yours.) The benefit is often positive because your customers know you care about their opinions, but you will need to act on their suggestions quickly.

When you have information which is not proprietary and would be useful to your customers, you may wish to share it. You particularly may want to share information if you have taken action based on input which your customers provided. It's extra work and costs a little more, but remember these people are not only the ones who "pay your bills"; they have also given you their time to talk about *your* business. These are relationships you want to enhance.

▼ UNDERSTANDING THE COMPETITION

It is especially important that you understand the strengths and weaknesses of your competition. Competitors' customers should be asked the same questions that you have asked of your customers. If you are conducting the survey of your own customers, this part of the research will have to be done by a third party. Try to ensure that the same questions are asked in the same way in which you have asked them.

If you learn that the competition is doing better than you in areas that could cause your customers to switch vendors, your action plans are clear. If you absolutely can't meet your competition, be honestly creative; change the "shape of the deal." Your immediate need is to work toward quantifying and taking actions concerning what you have learned. It is necessary to address your own customers' issues and also counteract in those areas where your competition is exceeding you.

Understanding customers' views of your competitors is there for the asking, but few ask.

▼ REQUESTING DATA FROM A RESEARCH FIRM

Generally, if you have worked with a market research firm, this firm is the best equipped to do the initial analysis of the results. It has conducted the study and understands the nuances. It should have the latest analytic tools at its disposal and will understand the ways in which the sample can be segmented to maintain validity. Also, returning to one of the reasons why we hire outsiders, a research firm is more objective about our business.

Even if the research firm does the analysis, you should request detailed backup data, although you probably will not want all the "raw data." Have you ever seen the raw data from an extensive survey? Raw data are the reams of output that constitute the basis of the crisp report on our desk. Raw data can be overwhelming to those who don't work with it daily. Although we certainly don't advise requesting all these data, we suggest that you obtain a disk or direct on-line access to specific detailed information. (Understand that the research firm will mask names of competitors and their customers and, when appropriate, your own customers as well. This is important to the integrity of the research process.)

The reasons you may want detailed backup data are

- Because your specific knowledge of the business may provide a different perspective from that of the research firm.
- To be sure you have a complete understanding of problem areas.
- To develop a model to allow you to examine the factors in different ways and their effects upon each other.
- To examine trends of how well you are doing from year to year by certain market segments.
- To use as a tool in structuring the next survey.
- To be able to blend and compare this information with other information such as market share.

This last point is important. Section 7.0 of the Malcolm Baldrige application requires evidence of integration of customer satisfaction information with other data; market share is designated specifically. If your satisfaction data show excellent ratings but your company is losing share, something is seriously wrong. Are you only measuring the loyal few who wouldn't think of "shopping" elsewhere? Survey those who have defected to help determine the problem.

▼ ANALYZING DATA

Whether you are actually analyzing the data or are critiquing the analysis, the first look at the results of a survey is very exciting. It's akin to seeing the ending of a sports event, reading the last pages of a book, or finding out, in the spring, which tulip bulbs the squirrels didn't manage to find.

Like the book ending, it may be bittersweet. It may also make you think of questions the author or, in this case, you didn't ask in the research procedure. Here are our cautions during the analysis process.

Eight Caveats or "Red Flags" in Analyzing Data

Red Flag 1. *You can't make the data answer a question that you didn't ask.*

We've seen people who say, "But we asked this question and that question. Doesn't that combination mean such and such?" Probably not; that's too risky an assumption. Just because your customers favor blue and red—both of which are primary colors—doesn't necessarily mean that they like yellow, the third primary color.

We hope this will underscore that the initial in-depth planning and interviews, which may seem time consuming and expensive, are worth it. If the beginning phase is thorough, it is less likely you will have questions at the end of your process that you wish you had asked.

Red Flag 2. *Typically, valid conclusions cannot be drawn from data which are segmented differently from the original sample design.*

Let's look at an example. As we examine interview results, we observe that responses in New England are different from those of the rest of the sample. We are planning an expansion in Massachusetts. Maybe that means that the Massachusetts market is different. Maybe? You need to look specifically at Massachusetts. Unless the initial segmentation was carefully done and you suspected possible geographical differences, you may not have a representative sample of New England let alone Massachusetts. Not all is lost. You may find that you have a sufficient sample or you can add to your sample. But that costs money, which is why it is better to proceed carefully at the outset. Not that everything will be right, but the odds are significantly better.

Red Flag 3. *Don't "force fit" data or stretch research results to prove a point.*

Someone in senior management has decided that your company is best-in-class in customized service. He or she asks you to prove this through your data. The questions really weren't that specific or the results don't really support this conclusion. This is tough, but we'd rather lose the possibility of a promotion over this one. Tell the story the way the data tell it. Once you begin tampering with the integrity of the information you transmit, *all* the information you transmit is at risk as well as *your* integrity.

Red Flag 4. *Don't assume an **average** score means that you are average.*

It's tempting to average the results. It's a relatively easy way to look at how well you did. Let's assume you have used a five-point scale with "5" being "excellent." When you average the results, it may show that you are just that, "average," that is, a "3." But, in fact you may have received all "5's" and all "1's" or all "2's" and all "4's." Exaggerated? Only a little. We've seen a number of instances where people didn't realize that they had *pockets of excellence* and *pockets of failure* because they didn't look at the distribution along each point on the scale. Look at each point on the scale. Pay attention to the precise distribution of the data.

Red Flag 5. *Be sure that the person who uses or attempts to use sophisticated analysis techniques understands the power and the limitations of those techniques.*

Although we need to be careful about looking for results which are not present, this is different from finding answers which are not apparent. There are a number of analytic techniques—multiple regression analysis, for example, which allow us to reach beyond the specific answers to the questions. Proper use of these techniques allows us to see interactions, find new interpretations, and possibly even isolate specific problems. But working with these statistical tools requires the skill of someone who truly understands how to do this. We highly recommend that you get this extra mileage from your research; but if you do not have the skill "in house," have your research firm or another skilled consultant do the analysis for you.

Red Flag 6. *If you "must" use data from a survey which is not up to date, proceed with caution. Try to validate the survey's present relevance and accuracy.*

Sometimes it is tempting when we don't have up-to-date information on hand to rely on results from "that survey" we (or someone else) conducted two or three years ago. It may still be valid, but the problem is, because we are using "facts," our colleagues may have too much confidence in its validity. It is possible that a brief telephone survey may confirm whether the data are still accurate and relevant.

Red Flag 7. *Don't view the research on a "stand-alone" basis only. Blend it with other information.*

Because time and cost constraints do not allow you to survey all your customers and all of your competitors, there will be some necessary shortcuts made when you structure the sample. The research firm will probably interview only your key competitors, for example. Remember to blend this analysis with information you may have about emerging competitors and potentially large customers. Be sure that you are aware when they should be included in your primary research effort. This applies to the results as well. These can be enriched by other insights about your customers and competitors.

Red Flag 8. *Look at data by customer or customers as well as frequency of need or occurrence.*

Many of your customers may need something critically, but they may need it only 2 percent of the time. Be careful that you don't view this as something that is only "2 percent important." This could be a clue to acquiring and maintaining customers and/or generating higher profits.

To understand this, it is necessary to analyze information by customer and by number of customers who have a specific need or concern, not only the frequency with which that need occurs. For example, in reviewing results, you may find that service beyond a certain hour is required only 5 percent of the time. With only this perspective, you are likely to decide that longer service hours are not required.

Reexamine the data by looking at each customer's response before you make that decision. It may be that 90 percent of your customers require longer service hours sometime during the year; it's just that they don't require it often. Could it also be that when they need the longer service hours, it is extremely critical? If so, this may prompt your customers to go elsewhere or cause serious dissatisfaction with which you may not be aware. For example, during the Christmas season, retailers whose stores close when their competitors are open are very likely to lose business. But, in this case, customers may not expect those longer service hours during other times of the year.

Where possible, evaluating data by customer is important. What are the requirements which seem to differ from customer to customer; what special services or additional hours should you provide?

A supplier we use for providing 35mm slides has a pricing scale which is based partially on the time which you allow them to deliver the slides to you. If their people have to work overtime, they pass along that cost plus a high markup to their customers. If we need those slides for tomorrow's presentation, of course, we are willing to pay the premium.

Table 2-1 Caveats in Analyzing Data

1. You can't make the data answer questions you didn't ask.

2. Typically, valid conclusions cannot be drawn from data that are segmented differently from the original sample design.

3. Don't "force fit" data or stretch results to prove a point.

4. Don't assume that an average score means that you are average.

5. Be sure that the person who utilizes sophisticated analysis techniques understands the power and limitations of those techniques.

6. If you "must" use information from a survey which is not up to date, proceed with caution; try to validate its present relevance and accuracy.

7. Don't view the research results on a stand-alone basis only; blend the results with other information.

8. Look at data by customer or customer segments as well as frequency of need or action.

Not only can these extras provide you with higher satisfaction levels, but you can frequently charge a higher rate during extended hours or for customized products or services.

▼ COMMUNICATING THE RESULTS TO ALL CONCERNED

If you have worked with a market research firm, it is usually advisable for the research firm to present results to management, but this varies with management style and expectations. Some companies prefer a member of their own staff to present to allow for a more open dialogue. Although you should understand the alternatives, you are the best judge of *who, what, where,* and *when* in terms of presentation of the findings.

Whether you have conducted the research or it was conducted by a third party, it is very important that the data are made known as soon as they are analyzed and available. Transmitting the information to those who can act upon it in a timely, appropriate manner is critical. Interim reviews should be conducted to provide immediate feedbacks on specific, serious customer problems.

With regard to any areas of dissatisfaction, discussions should be held with responsible managers as soon as possible. Ultimately, it is very important that you have all the backup data with regard to key problems which have surfaced. Be sure that the responsible managers have a complete understanding of an issue prior to any "open forum" presentation of the information. They will want time to think and be able to respond with plans for corrective action.

We would like to hang banners everywhere that say

Bad news is not the end of your business success. However, not knowing the bad news and not taking corrective actions may be.

Too often, the messenger is silenced when in fact he or she should be applauded. Those who take effective corrective action procedures should be applauded even more loudly.

Make sure that departments or geographic areas which have done particularly well get recognition. Remember this is *customer* **satisfaction** *research*, not *dissatisfaction*. Also, remember that people are unique and people have different ways of transmitting their ideas.

Be sure that management is aware of the jobs well done and recognize those people who have done the work.

Your research will now provide the following:

- *The Base for Trend Analysis.* This is just the starting point of what should be an ongoing customer satisfaction survey process. Customer satisfaction research should be conducted regularly. In most cases, this is an annual activity. Dependent on the volatility of your market, annually may not be adequate. A number of companies interview monthly.

  The questionnaire should be relatively the same and should be administered in the same way to ensure validity of comparisons from year to year (or quarter to quarter or month to month). We say relatively the same because as it becomes evident that your marketplace is changing, you may need to add or delete factors.

- *Basis for Prioritizing Actions for Improvement.* Since you now know the factors your customers consider important, how important they are relative to each other, and where you are weak in serving your customers relative to competition, your priorities for making improvements should be clear.

- *Keys to Setting Goals.* Your customers have now told you their expectations and how you are performing. From this, you will be able to set goals. In our chapter on benchmarking and setting goals, we use a specific example of using customer satisfaction research for setting goals.

▼ CONTINUALLY TALKING TO YOUR CUSTOMERS ABOUT IMPROVEMENT

When you have completed your first survey and taken appropriate actions for improvement, it should lead to improved total customer satisfaction for your company. But the process takes time; it takes time to measure, it takes time to make improvements, and it takes time for customers to recognize those improvements.

And it requires continuous action. Continue talking to your customers; listen to what they have to say and give them many reasons to want to do business with you. Let your customers know when you have made improvements. Whenever possible, make your customers your partners. Let them help you create your total quality process. Through this, you can outlast and outperform all your competitors!

In summary

- Talk to your front-line people about their customer interfaces.
- Correctly identify your customers, including all customer types.
- Determine the objectives of your research and prepare a discussion guide to use when interviewing.
- Conduct personal interviews with your customers to understand their overall requirements.
- Determine what factors are important to customers.
- Determine how customers rank the important factors.
- Learn where customers "set the bars" of excellence.
- Develop the sample and the questionnaire for quantifiable research using results from the personal interviews.
- Conduct quantifiable research interviews.
- Be careful in analyzing the results. (Data play tricks.)

- Communicate the news. (Don't kill messengers.)
- Develop action plans and set goals for improvement based on data.
- Remember that the process is iterative, but may need recalibration based on marketplace changes.
- Working with a market research firm is advisable for objectivity, expertise, and competitive access.

CHAPTER THREE

How to Listen to Your Employees and Help Them Focus on the Customer

A leader's job is to absorb pain, not to inflict it.

MAX DUPREE, CEO,
Herman Miller Corporation

By now, it should be obvious that "getting started" requires a great deal of preparation. We've discussed the role of quality champions and the importance of understanding your customers. Now, we'll focus on the third part of our quality process: understanding your employees.

Without the full participation and support of your employees, total quality cannot be achieved. It is the role of the leader to not only champion quality, but to provide the vision, direction, resources, and moral support that enables his or her people to succeed. As Paul Mosher, President of Kelco, the San Diego-based division of Merck & Co., Inc., told us, "Without the untiring patience of senior management, the quality process is going nowhere!" Mosher added that "Kelco has been at it for four years and, just now, the quality improvement seeds we planted four years ago are beginning to sprout within our company's culture." A meaningful quality process requires a long-term commitment and patience from all employees. To be successful, it must permeate the culture of an organization.

So how can you ensure that your company's quality process enjoys the support of your employees? One way this can be accomplished is to examine your organization from the inside out, and ask yourself, "What do my people need to do their jobs to the best of their ability—and be assured they will succeed?" The challenge is to find the means that will ensure a positive outcome.

It is the *human dimension* first and foremost that managers must understand to succeed in implementing a quality process. We emphasize the human dimension because people ultimately control the quality process. Every employee in your organization has unique needs and requirements that must be met if they are to succeed at their jobs. This holds true regardless of your service, product, or the structure of your company.

For example, employees' work environments directly affect their productivity. Consider bank tellers who must be able to concentrate on each transaction. It would be disruptive and imprudent to pipe heavy metal rock music throughout the bank lobby. It might cause you to lose a few older customers as well! On the other hand, rock music might increase the productivity of a nightclub waitress or a construction paint crew.

Let's examine a brief checklist of six areas which managers should consider in relation to their employees.

1. *Team Objectives*. Are they linked to your company's overall mission and objectives?

2. *Personality Match*. Do organizational changes, hiring procedures, and training include the consideration of employees working well together?

3. *Workplace Environment*. Is it soundproofed when required? Do you prefer private offices or an open bay space plan? Do you want a no smoking environment? And so on.

4. *Office Equipment*. Is it functional or outdated? Does it retard and inhibit productivity or aid it?

5. *Dress Codes.* How do you want your customers to perceive your company image? How will a dress code stimulate or diminish employees' self-image on the job?

6. *Policies and Empowerment*. Do your employees have flexibility and authority to act, or are their hands tied due to rigid policies and chain-of-command decision making?

▼ A COMMITMENT TO QUALITY BRINGS ABOUT CHANGE

We've said that before *change* can happen within an organization, people must believe that change is possible. Believing that change is possible is an essential first step to instituting a total quality process.

Sometimes managers waste energy trying to convince people that change is *not* possible. A group of managers in China in 1989 believed that they knew best and did not institute the changes which their employees felt were necessary. The consequences were exceedingly harsh. The following is an excerpt from an article entitled "Chinese Managers Executed" which appeared in *The Wall Street Journal* on October 17, 1989.

▼ MANAGERS EXECUTED FOR SHODDY QUALITY WORK

(Bejing)—Eighteen factory managers were executed for poor product quality at Chien Bien Refrigerator Factory on the outskirts of the Chinese capital. The managers, including the plant manager, the quality control manager, the engineering managers and their top staff, were taken to a rice paddy outside the factory and unceremoniously shot to death as 500 plant workers looked on.

Minister of Economic Reform spokesman Xi Ten Haun said the action was required for committing unpardonable crimes against the people of China. He blamed the managers for ignoring quality and forcing shoddy work, saying the factory's output of refrigerators had a reputation for failure. For years, factory workers complained that many component parts did not meet specification and the end product did not function as required. Complaining workers quoted the plant manager as saying,

"Ship it!" Refrigerators are among the most sought-after consumer items in China. Customers, who waited up to five years for their appliances, were outraged at the inferior quality.

"It is understandable that our citizens would express shock and outrage when managers are careless in their attitudes towards the welfare of others," Haun said. "Our soldiers are justified in wishing to bring proper justice to those errant managers."

While the punishment of execution by firing squad certainly goes far beyond the norm for curbing poor quality and service, we some-times wonder why it is that more frustrated employees and customers haven't taken to the streets and demanded that managers—like those at the refrigerator factory—are, at least, held accountable for their actions.

▼ WHY MANAGEMENT SHOULD LISTEN TO ITS EMPLOYEES

Earlier, we addressed the importance of listening to your customer-con-tact employees for their input on customers' requirements. We also want to stress that it is important to listen to your employees about potential failure in products or processes that, ultimately, may inhibit your suc-cess.

This was the tragic lesson NASA learned in 1986 when the space shuttle, *Challenger*, exploded shortly after its launch due to faulty O-rings. As the full story came to light, it was discovered that several engineers, who worked for the supplier firm that manufactured the O-rings, had questioned the quality and reliability of their O-ring product. But management was not responsive and discounted the engineers' concerns. This failure by management to listen to its em-ployees contributed to America's worst space disaster, killing seven astronauts.

You not only need to give your employees the appropriate respon-sibility, but also the authority to improve your products and customer service. When you send your people mixed messages that translate into "quality is important, but short-term profits—not customers' and employees' concerns—are management's primary focus," your employees will become malcontents. Their dissatisfaction with the company will undermine management's objectives and, ultimately, become visible to your customers. At first, this air of discontent may take the form of subtle dissatisfaction. It may be noted in arguments where strong, vocal differences of opinion are aired. But eventually, employees—if not listened to and respected for their views—will become defiant of company policy, which they deem to be wrong, and become openly disrespectful of management's decisions.

Consider these two examples we encountered in our research. A plant manager described to us her predicament with senior management's contradictory message, which was, "Yes, we want the best quality in construction, but don't fall behind in your production quotas or shipping the product!" When push came to shove, the plant manager sacrificed quality rather than run the risk of losing her job because her production quota was behind an unrealistic schedule. Therefore, orders of consistent quality couldn't be shipped on time. It is likely, in this case, that product was sent back and the problem had to be corrected later, causing more cost as well as customer dissatisfaction. Many young managers state, "Why is it we are often not allowed an adequate schedule to do it right the first time, but there is always time to do it again?"

Our second example is somewhat more subtle. A corporate vice president of sales directed his retail clothing outlets to stock a particular leather jacket and actively promote it—even though the quality of leather was inferior—and this had been reported up the chain to headquarters. Nevertheless, the directive was issued a second time, and each outlet was expected to sell its inventory.

Later, when several sales associates in the Southeast region, were talking shop, the issue of the "inferior-quality" leather jackets was raised. Several sales associates stated that they advised customers "not to buy the jacket because it wouldn't last." In other words, they ignored management's bad decision and simply went about business as usual.

Whenever possible, employees should raise issues such as inferior products to management and discuss their feelings and differences. But, as we have seen, some managements do not react positively to this. It is destructive to the quality process for management to send mixed messages or dictate policies and rules that compromise employees. Employees need clear direction and open communication, or they, particularly those who are most capable and customer oriented, are likely to leave.

As one 1991 study by the Customer Relations Institute revealed, 18 percent of the dissatisfied employees who were surveyed stated that they left their company because they were uncomfortable about enforcing rules and procedures that they felt were not in their customers' best interest.

One way to counter this situation is to institute an assessment plan as part of your total quality process. We define this internal assessment as *a measurement process in which you determine the needs and attitudes of your employees.* The key question that we are trying to answer is: "How well do we serve those employees whom we rely on to serve our customers and who rely on us to set the standards?"

▼ PREPARING FOR THE ASSESSMENT PHASE

Before you begin your assessment program, employees must be convinced that management has made a long-term commitment to them and to the quality process. Management—through its words and actions—must have demonstrated to employees that they are the company's greatest asset and that they have demonstrated total commitment to its internal and external customers. This can be done by removing unfriendly policies and rules that alienate or intimidate customers, empowering employees to make decisions that "save the day" for customers, and by treating employees and customers with dignity and respect.

Once employees see management "walking their talk," they will begin to challenge their own attitudes and behaviors and, eventually, change the way they treat customers and their fellow employees. The result will be a better understanding of your quality process and a stronger commitment to the vision and values that management espouses.

We think Dr. Ken Blanchard captured the feeling when he said, "Catch me doing something right!" Pride yourself on acknowledging lots of little things your people are doing right. Resist the temptation to "knock heads" when someone fails to meet your expectations. Frankly, we have found that "restraint" and "patience" are the two most difficult lessons managers must master in order to keep from self-destructing their quality process! Think about it: to bruise the ego of an employee or pour salt in the wounds of someone who messed up only stalls your quality process. No good can possibly come from it. The employee will be upset and you'll be upset. Suddenly, barriers will be erected between you and the rest of your employees because many of them will side with the employee as the underdog. After all, they know how it feels to work for someone who doesn't appreciate them!

You need to determine if there are barriers to your employees' being easily able to talk honestly about their suggestions for improvements. If your company lacks the full faith, confidence, and trust of its employees, you will never get below the superficial response level in your assessment process.

If you need to "test the water," on whether your employees feel they can talk openly about needed improvements in your company, we suggest that you work with a few key, trusted employees who have a good rapport with many people in the company. Ask them if there are unresolved issues that need to be addressed and deal with these unresolved issues before you begin. Alternatively, you can have a third party conduct an anonymous survey which deals with employee attitudes about raising issues and concerns. Once you are convinced that employees believe that you will honor their suggestions and criticisms, you can begin your assessment.

▼ THE ASSESSMENT PROCESS

The assessment begins with scheduling meetings with your employees to get their input on what's going right and what's going wrong in the company. By arranging them as breakfast or lunch meetings, you can minimize employees' time away from their functions and help create an informal atmosphere. We suggest small groups of six to eight people. Several of these or more can be run in the same week or month depending on the size of your company. Continue to conduct these meetings on a regular basis.

Each meeting should have a specific agenda and focus. When a meeting is scheduled, the attendees should be informed of the agenda of that particular meeting. An example of a particular month's focus or theme is: "How do we improve our employee suggestion system?"

The moderator of these meetings can vary based on the theme. Often people from Human Resources or Education & Training are effective initial moderators because of their training and their knowledge of the issues that are particularly related to employee development. At the outset and on an ongoing basis, however, you will want to cover three key broad issues. These are:

1. What is our company doing right?

2. What is our company doing wrong?

3. What policies, procedures, rules, or programs should be reviewed, altered, enforced, deleted, or added to make our company a better place to work as well as a more quality driven, customer-focused environment?

We recommend that the moderator:

- Encourage all employees to be involved and open. Ensure that when criticisms are made they are recorded, and that the tone of the meeting is returned to a positive, "How do we correct this?" attitude.

- Ask someone to be the recorder (using a flip chart is a good way to do this). As the recorder writes, the moderator should concentrate on the content of the discussion and "ask for examples" and "tell me mores."

- Focus on one issue at a time. If someone addresses another topic before it is timely, ask the recorder to note that, and come back to it later.

- Summarize and develop actions for improvement.

- Communicate back to employees and let them know that they will be part of the improvement process.

- Communicate to appropriate managers any issues which will require their support.

▼ QUALITY ACTION TEAMS

Once a number of groups have met, their responses can be combined to provide an overall view of the issues that need to be addressed first; also, groups which seem to have similar concerns can be identified.

The groups which have similar concerns should be formed into teams. We call them quality action teams (QATs). Not too long ago, we would have recommended that these teams should be in the same department or related departments, work in the same shift, and certainly be in the same physical location. Consistency of these factors makes communications much easier. However, we now know from recent experiences that cross-functional, even cross-locational, cross-divisional teams not only work, but also can create solutions with much greater impact. The team's commonality should be its members' interest in a particular issue and their willingness to find a solution to a specific problem.

These quality action teams should be empowered to solve the problem and be given the resources to do so. They may need training in problem-solving techniques and guidance in such things as setting up and running meetings. Provide them with this assistance and any other required guidance. Since the group identified the problem, it is possible that they already feel a responsibility for finding a solution.

Let the team members know that it is their responsibility to find the root cause of the problem, to analyze the problem, to come up with the optimal solution, and where feasible, to implement that solution. Be sure to also let them know that you will guide them when they need help.

A piece of advice we heard recently from a Disney manager was this: "Any problem that is man-made can be fixed by mankind." We agree. As a leader and quality champion, you must encourage your QATs to succeed. Assist them in sticking to the central problem and in evaluating alternative solutions to that problem. The key is to help the team understand their primary mission—to fix the problem; remind them that they don't need to fix the universe.

Ask for monthly status reports from each of the teams and determine what support they need. As they solve one problem, let them determine another one to tackle. New problems will also emerge as moderators continue to hold assessment meetings.

Always publicize QAT outcomes. If a policy or operating method cannot be changed, communicate this to the team immediately. These important steps build trust and encourage participation in the future. Finally, celebrate your quality improvement successes. Recognize the accomplishments of those champions who volunteered to solve a problem or resolve an issue.

▼ HOW THE RITZ-CARLTON HOTELS INVITES EMPLOYEE PARTICIPATION IN THE QUALITY IMPROVEMENT PROCESS

One company that has gained an international reputation for quality and service, and also practices a variation of this assessment plan, is Ritz-Carlton Hotels. Headquartered in Atlanta, Ritz-Carlton is renowned for outstanding service and enjoys a reputation as the finest hotel company in the United States. As a recipient of the 1992 Malcolm Baldrige National Quality Award, the Ritz-Carlton Hotels clearly demonstrated that outstanding quality and guest service can be quantified in a service business and made part of its everyday mission. The Ritz-Carlton has raised the performance bar not only for all hotels but also for other service companies. (See Figure 3-1 on page 74.)

In today's customer-fickle world, the Ritz-Carlton is highly sensitive to the whims and idiosyncrasies of its guests. Each hotel has trained its employees to be alert throughout the day for any physical plant improvements or service glitches they might notice. Whether an employee works in housekeeping, security, or convention services, everyone is expected to offer daily suggestions on how their property and operations can be improved.

Interestingly, however, Ritz-Carlton Hotels goes one step better than most hotel companies. When an employee observes a "defect," he or she "describes the problem or condition that caused an internal or external customer to be dissatisfied" on a formal report. The report is called the Internal Defect Report/*Reporte de los Defectos Internos*. (See Figure 3-2 on pages 75-76.)

Space is provided on the back side of the report for the hotel's Executive Committee to track and follow up on each report that is filed. The management team at Ritz-Carlton Hotels follows a 24/30/48 response formula. A response from someone of the management team is due within 24 hours of the report being submitted. Within 30 hours, management verifies the effectiveness of a solution. Within 48 hours, an action plan has been developed to solve the problem or at least begin to address it.

Consider the number of reports filed each week by Ritz-Carlton's 400 employees and the time it takes to address each and every one of them by management. It's this attention to detail and the quantification of the most serious and costly problems and fixing them right the first time that makes The Ritz-Carlton exceptional!

Unfortunately, many people can recall countless times they complained to the front desk at the XYZ Hotel about a broken alarm clock, a door key or lock problem, or the lack of hot water in the bathroom, only to check out three days later and nothing was fixed. Still worse, a colleague told us about his stay at one upscale hotel in Bethesda, Maryland, where he had experienced a plumbing problem only to

The Ritz-Carlton
CREDO

The Ritz-Carlton Hotel is a place where the genuine care and comfort of our guests is our highest mission.

We pledge to provide the finest personal service and facilities for our guests who will always enjoy a warm, relaxed yet refined ambience.

The Ritz-Carlton experience enlivens the senses, instills well-being, and fulfills even the unexpressed wishes and needs of our guests.

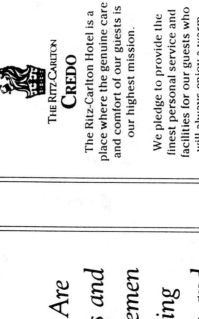

"We Are Ladies and Gentlemen Serving Ladies and Gentlemen"

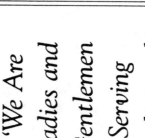

THREE STEPS OF SERVICE

1

A warm and sincere greeting. Use the guest name, if and when possible.

2

Anticipation and compliance with guest needs.

3

Fond farewell. Give them a warm good-bye and use their names, if and when possible.

Figure 3-1 Ritz-Carlton Performance Criteria
Source: Ritz-Carlton Hotels

THE RITZ-CARLTON
HOTEL COMPANY

INTERNAL DEFECT REPORT
REPORTE DE LOS DEFECTOS INTERNOS

Name *Nombre:* _____

Department *Departamento:* _____

Date *Fecha:* _____

**Please describe any problem or condition you experience that
causes either internal or external customers to be dissatisfied.**

*Por favor, de dar la descripcion de cualquier problema o condicion que
Usted ha visto que puede ser la causa de que un huespede o empleado no se conforma.*

Problem *Problema:* please specify "what", "when" and "to whom" *especificamente "que", "cuando" y "a quien"*

_____

_____

_____

_____

_____

_____

_____

_____

Possible Cause *Posible Causa:* _____

_____

_____

Recommended Solution *Solucion Recomendada:* _____

_____

_____

Has this problem occurred before? *¿Ha ocurrido el mismo problema otra veces?* _____

If "yes", how often does it occur? *En caso afirmativo, ¿cuantas veces?*   _____ times a day   *veces al dia*

_____ times a week   *veces a la semana*

_____ times a month *veces al mes*

Figure 3-2 Ritz-Carlton Internal Defect Report

EXECUTIVE COMMITTEE
TRACKING AND FOLLOW-UP

To be completed by member of the Executive Committee

Delegate to handle defect: _____

Please complete the following date:

    Submitted by employee: _____

    Received by Executive Committee: _____

    Responded to employee: _____   24

    Developed ACTION PLAN: _____   48

    Implemented ACTION PLAN: _____

    Verified effectiveness of solution: _____   30

    Standardized the solution: _____

Any additional information about the defect: _____

_____

_____

_____

_____

_____

_____

Description of the ACTION PLAN:_____

_____

_____

_____

_____

_____

_____

Figure 3-2 Ritz-Carlton Internal Defect Report, continued

return the next week, be assigned the same room, and (surprise!) the problem still had not been fixed. He immediately phoned the front desk and *demanded* a new room where the plumbing worked! Needless to say, he never returned to that hotel.

At the Ritz-Carlton Hotels, of course, this kind of recurring problem doesn't happen for two reasons. First, employees are empowered to respond quickly and decisively to every kind of customer complaint or concern. Second, the Internal Defect Report/*Reporte de los Defectos Internos* is treated as a golden opportunity to avert customer dissatisfaction.

We share these stories to reinforce the point that employees will uphold your quality standards as well as your commitment to customer satisfaction, provided you do six things:

1. Lead by example.

2. Ensure that your people are familiar with how their roles affect internal and external customer satisfaction.

3. Communicate your company's mission and goals to all employees.

4. Invite all employees to play a role in your company's commitment to quality by involving them in the total quality process.

5. Listen to employee suggestions and act swiftly on them.

6. Reward employees for their contributions to quality improvement.

▼ SEEING YOUR EMPLOYEES AS INTERNAL CUSTOMERS

Not all of your customers are external. Remember that employees are customers to each other. Almost every employee serves an *internal customer*—or a fellow employee. Many of these internal customers/employees, in turn, serve *external* customers, that is, the end users and buyers of your products or services.

Improvement of internal service is very important beyond the fact that improvement makes internal service faster, more accurate, or otherwise better. Improvement of internal service positively affects employee morale and enhances your service to your customers. Those savings that you make internally will ultimately be seen externally as well.

Internal supplier groups can determine their customers' level of satisfaction using a process which is similar to the one that we discussed in the previous chapter. We have found that measuring internal customer satisfaction is very similar to measuring external customer satisfaction. That is, internal suppliers should ask their customers what factors are important to them and then measure their customers' satisfaction with those factors.

Since internal customers and their internal suppliers work with each other on a regular basis, it is relatively easy to conduct a survey of "What is important?" and "Where do we need to improve?" But it requires discipline to carry this out. Time for this procedure must be scheduled and honored. Otherwise, day-to-day concerns will always take precedence.

Measuring internal customer satisfaction is necessary because it provides rich new insights into processes which have become rote. Additionally, it is important because it's the "customer" telling the "supplier" what's wrong—not the employee telling the manager or the manager telling his or her staff—it has a more powerful and less controversial impact.

Often your *internal* customers may not have a choice about doing business with you. This can be a significant difference. How well you perform as an internal supplier is directly related to your motivation in understanding and reacting to your *internal* customers' requirements.

Initially, ask the same questions you would ask of your external customers, questions such as, "What do you like best about dealing with us?" and "What do you like least about dealing with us?" will get you straightforward answers. In one instance, when an internal customer was buying services from another division, the internal customer was asked, "What do you like least about dealing with us?" The supplier was surprised and stunned by the answer. The customer told him, "You are arrogant." Only then did the internal supplier realize how easy it is to fall into the trap of becoming arrogant when you subconsciously know that "you're the only game in town." And, because of this "limited-options" relationship, his customer was willing to put up with more grief and displeasure than would normally be acceptable.

Ultimately, this arrogant attitude filters across the organization and becomes visible to *external* customers. Head it off at the pass! Measure internal-to-internal transactions on a regular basis. Make sure these transactions are working smoothly (according to your *customers' standards*, not yours, of course!). If they are not flowing smoothly, you run the risk that your external customers will receive second-class treatment. It is likely to happen because it will become "the accepted practice"—"the way things are done." If you do not challenge destructive behavioral tendencies, they will take root and flourish, undermining your long-term customer relations.

The risk of second-class service permeating your company is not the only negative factor you face. *Doing things the wrong way the first time costs money!* Internal customers who receive flawed staff work must redo this work. That effort costs you time, energy, and money! Not only that, it ultimately will affect morale, especially if management allows inferior work to continue unchallenged.

▼ WHY PEOPLE DON'T COMPLAIN

Studies reveal that only 4 percent of your dissatisfied customers will take the time to complain. We believe that this applies to your employees as well as your external customers. There are a number of reasons why both customers and employees are reluctant to complain. Some of the key reasons are the following:

1. *It's not worth the hassle.* "My time is too valuable and complaining is a hassle," is how most people feel. Both employees and customers will drop the incident and just get on with their lives. For the most part, people are tolerant and have an amazing ability to shrug off bad service or poor quality. When it reaches the boiling point, however, they'll seek alternative places to work or conduct their business. And, by the way, don't expect a postcard from them telling you *why* they left.

2. People don't believe complaining will do any good. They're right! For example, if you tell a checker in a grocery store that the check out lane is too slow or comment to the produce clerk that the Boston lettuce looks wilted, they aren't likely to share your comments with the store manager.

If you complain to your boss about something that isn't within her immediate control, she isn't likely to share your story with her boss. Most people don't like bad news. We've been conditioned at an early age that "bad news messengers" get slain. Whistleblowers rank very low on the popularity scale. So, at some point, we stop communicating the problem and just ignore it or go around it.

3. People don't know where to complain or how to file a complaint. If you slip your card into the automatic teller machine (ATM) and the machine malfunctions and gobbles up your card, what can you do? Have you ever tried to reach a real person on the ATM phone line, let alone on Saturday morning? If you're not able to break through that bureaucratic maze, how do you proceed? Yet, this does not have to be the case; we applaud the STAR system where they have gotten it right the first time.

4. People fear retaliation or revenge. Imagine this unpleasant scenario:

Scene One: A business traveler arrives at the Pittsburgh airport and checks his bag to Rochester, *Minnesota.* Unfortunately, when he arrives in Minnesota, he learns his bags are on their way to Rochester, *New York!* An honest mistake by the skycap or airline's counter agent, you say? Tell that to the flabbergasted passenger who had his meeting materials and business attire packed away for that all-important client presentation. A business traveler doesn't want excuses; he wants results—and fast!

Scene Two: Our frustrated passenger is directed to the baggage claim counter by a disinterested employee. There the passenger finds himself arguing over company policy with an airline baggage claim representative who was carefully taught to enforce the airline's rules and procedures for missing baggage. The employee tells the distraught passenger that it was the customer's responsibility to check the baggage claim ticket before leaving the airline counter in Pittsburgh. By now, the passenger is infuriated and having great difficulty remaining calm. He considers his options—legal action against the airline, nasty letters, suicide! The passenger wants to register a complaint but suspects his bag may end up in Hong Kong, never to be seen again. In the end, the customer silently vows never to fly that airline again.

Meanwhile, the airline baggage claim representative is also frustrated. This awkward situation occurs repeatedly. The airline's policies get in the way of his really helping customers. And, while the employee wants to escalate his concerns, he knows that these are *management's* policies. He fears that any suggestions to management might be interpreted the wrong way and could affect his chances for a promotion if he tries to buck the system. Maybe, if he's lucky, he can get a job at Scandinavian Airlines System where he has heard from their employees and passengers that the *customer comes first* and baggage claim issues are resolved more easily because employees are empowered to act immediately on behalf of its customers.

▼ REVIEWING EMPLOYEES' JOB FUNCTIONS AND TRACKING THEIR PROFESSIONAL DEVELOPMENT

Another important dimension of understanding your employees is to review each employee's job function to determine exactly what jobs and tasks he or she performs. In this context, we define job function as the *primary duties each employee performs.*

A word of caution is required here. The job the person was hired for may, in fact, be different from the job the person is performing. If the job has evolved beyond the description, be sure to update the job description so that the person is being recognized and evaluated for the things he or she is really doing as opposed to evaluating based on an outdated job description. This is particularly critical as companies evolve to more team-oriented environments and empowerment.

The easiest way to determine the employee's *job function* is to ask, "How do you spend most of your day?" Capture the major responses in order to understand what the job description should really say. Also, determine how these activities relate directly or indirectly to customer satisfaction or the profitability of the company. It may be that most of the function has lost its value and is no longer necessary.

One management responsibility that is often overlooked is evaluating jobs and developing the talent in their departments in terms of the jobs that need to be done. The fact that a company has honest, dedicated, and well-intentioned people who are *not* performing vital roles is not their fault. It is a management problem. It is management's job to challenge these employees, retrain them if necessary, and put them to work in meaningful jobs.

This leads us to a second important aspect of understanding your people. As managers, and quality champions, it is essential to help your employees establish professional development goals.

To earn the trust of employees, managers must do everything within their power to develop their greatest asset—their people. Management must take responsibility for excellence and ensure that their employees keep pace with the rest of the business world in terms of their commitment to quality and service performance.

▼ LONG-TERM PROFESSIONAL DEVELOPMENT— THE KEY TO GROWTH

Ask employees whether their professional development goals are on track. Ask them how you can support their ongoing training and education. Develop a customized curriculum for each of your employees that is tailored to their specific goals and monitor their progress.

Develop long-term development plans for each employee. We encourage both group and individual interviews with your employees at each level. These can reap a great deal of useful information that goes far beyond the job function.

In group interviews, encourage your employees to talk first about their positive on-the-job experiences. Allow them to feel good about who they are, where they work, and the jobs they perform before you ask them to evaluate and perhaps criticize the system. Make sure you encourage everyone to participate.

Since some employees may not want to get involved, introduce a game approach to encourage responses from everyone. One exercise that we use is to have the class facilitator ask everyone to write down three things they love about their jobs. The facilitator gives the group time to swap answers with each other and then records these so that all can see them. The most popular answer gets a token prize. Also, the most unique answer wins a token prize. Repeat the exercise for "things I dislike about my job" or "things we can improve at our company." Promise anonymity and honor that promise. Failure to do so will destroy the trust and sabotage the entire process.

In individual interviews, be sure that you have a complete resume of each employee's background and that you understand his or her special skills and talents. This can be a win-win situation. As an example, your International Group may be desperately looking for someone fluent in Portuguese. Using this documentation, you can identify the best qualified potential candidate providing a benefit to him or her and to your International Group. After reviewing and documenting the employee's skills proceed to discuss the employee's goals and what he or she is doing to achieve both their own and the company's goals. Determine what training the company could offer to help them. Specifically ask:

1. What training and skills are required for you to perform your jobs?
2. What training and education do you already possess?
3. What training areas could the company offer that would help you excel in your jobs?

Ideally, your Education & Training Department has asked these questions and has tailored the programs accordingly. If not, through this process, you will be able to learn whether there are deficiencies in your company's training program. This can help in the development of a revised training plan. Best-in-class companies take action based on suggestions their employees share during these sessions.

We believe that corporate trainers and educators need to reexamine their menu of training programs and eliminate those items that do not complement the growth and development of internal customers/employees. We also believe that trainers need to take on the added role and responsibility of "corporate counselors." As corporate counselors, their primary job is to guide their internal customers to higher levels of professionalism and competence.

This means that the present training curriculum must be scrutinized and, in some cases, scrapped. Rather than offer the same old nebulous training classes that contribute little or nothing to the long-term quality results of a company or its people, training curriculums must be examined in terms of goals and objectives of the company and the needs of employees and their managers.

After you have met with employees in feedback sessions or department groups, and you've conducted surveys in every department, discuss employees' specific training needs with the appropriate department managers. Remember to listen for *causes, not symptoms.*

Michalak and Yager in *Making the Training Process Work* talk about concerns in this regard: "The manager who identifies a problem in the department is often talking about symptoms rather than causes. It would be foolhardy for the trainer to design, develop, and conduct a training program based *only* on the manager's perception of what is needed."

This is why employee interviews are important. They provide you with a balanced perspective. Our experience has been that a number of managers tie most employee-related problems to an employee's performance or attitude. This may or may not be justified. The problem may be lack of understanding of the job function, lack of training, or a poorly designed training program.

The problem could also be a procedural or policy-related issue. And despite the good intentions of a manager to fix the problem by sending the employee off to training, when the employee returns the problem will still exist if the system is at fault. In other words, the employee's work environment must complement your training efforts.

▼ POLICIES AND PROCEDURES THAT AFFECT EMPLOYEES AND CUSTOMERS ADVERSELY

Throughout this chapter, we mentioned the possibility of policies and procedures getting in the way of employees' providing good service to customers.

We recall one Hollywood movie example that serves as an excellent example of what we mean by "restrictive internal policies and practices" even though this Hollywood scene demonstrates how enforcement of company rules "saved the day" at a bank. Perhaps you remember the scene. It comes from the movie *Take the Money and Run*.

In this particular scene, a would-be robber named Virgil enters a bank and gives the bank teller a "stickup" note. The teller has trouble reading Virgil's scribble and asks him to interpret the note. Here's how the script flows:

Teller: *What does this say?*

Virgil: *Ugh . . . can't you read it?*

Teller: *No, I can't read this.*

Virgil: *Ugh . . . it says, "I am pointing a gun at you."*

Teller   (looking at the stickup note): *That looks like "gub." That doesn't look like gun.*

Virgil: *No, no that . . . that's gun, g-u-n.*

The argument continues and, finally, the teller calls another employee to interpret the note. Eventually, the teller says, "Oh, I see . . . this is a holdup," then asks, "May I see your gun?" The discussion between the tellers and Virgil continues much to his frustration:

Teller:	*Well, you'll have to have this note initialed by one of our vice presidents before I can give you any money.*
Virgil:	*Please. I'm in a rush.*
Teller:	*I'm sorry, but that's our policy . . . please see the gentleman in the grey suit.*

Subsequently, the bank vice president has everyone in the bank trying to decipher Virgil's note. Finally, Virgil is arrested in the bank by the police and sentenced to 800 years in the state penitentiary for attempted armed robbery!

While this Hollywood example may appear absurd, there is an essence of truth. There are illogical, rigid policies which have victimized almost all of us. When you audit your policies, you're likely to find some that are seriously destructive to your business. Conversely, there are valuable policies and procedures—the kind that protect your employees and/or your customers.

Unfortunately, too many policies, rules, and procedures are very outdated and overly restrictive. They squash creativity, inhibit customer satisfaction, and impede your quality process. Listen to your employees' comments in this regard. Also do an audit of all your major policies and procedures to determine whether they merit review and change. Put them on trial for their life.

Another example which is also absurd—but this one is true—is an incident that happened to our friends Sally and Charlie. One winter evening they had a craving for ice cream cones. Since it was winter they weren't surprised when there were no other customers in the ice cream store. They browsed for a few minutes among the variety of flavors and then were ready to make their selection.

Behind the counter were a teenager and her manager. When they went to place their order at the counter, the teenager said, "I'm sorry, you'll have to take a number." They looked at each other dumbfounded considering the fact that they were the only customers in the ice cream store. Sally said, "You're joking, of course!" But much to their chagrin, the teenager wasn't joking. She responded, "I'm sorry, it's our company policy; everyone must take a number before they can be served."

Charlie jumped into the absurd situation by saying, "Hey, we're the only customers in here! Why do we need a number?" To this the teenager sheepishly said, "Please, don't get me fired, my manager is watching!" At this point, they dutifully took their numbers. Sally was number 28 and Charlie was number 29. They looked up at the number board which stood at 25. As if she were a robot, the teenager dutifully called out "Number 26, number 27, number 28." When Sally's number was called, the teenager said, "May I take your order?" But Sally stated that at this point she had decided that hot chocolate sounded much better; she looked at Charlie and they left the store never to return.

Our friends' story is a clear case of how a company's well-intentioned effort to serve each customer in an orderly fashion can be misinterpreted and abused when it isn't coupled with adequate flexibility for allowing employees to adapt to the circumstances. Think of the burdens that policies like this one in the ice cream store place on your employees.

▼ CHANGING POLICIES AND PROCEDURES

We believe that there are three key ways to deal with policies that inhibit customer satisfaction. We recommend the following:

1. Delete them.

2. Alter them. (Get front-line employee and customer input on this.)

3. Empower your employees to waive them whenever appropriate.

Changing policies, rules, and procedures—as hard as it may seem—is the easy part of creating a quality process because policies exist in black and white, ready for your review. They can be modified by the stroke of a pen in most cases. But the more difficult transitions are those which deal with employee mind-sets and rigid management positions. We're referring to those ideas that are ingrained because of a potentially toxic attitude that is best described by that old refrain, "That's the way we've always done business around here!"

Very often, we fail to see things in the same light as our customers. We naturally view our methods through biased frames of references which have become clouded and obscured by our own life experiences as well as the corporate culture we work in. But our biased interpretations often go unnoticed and unchallenged because they have accumulated gradually over the years and become part of our core behavior. Ultimately, they affect not only our customers but our employee morale.

Make an irrevocable commitment to understand your employees' and customers' requirements with an objective to grow a quality-driven company. Then, design a quality process that will ensure your long-term success. Closely examine your internal policies and procedures because they are often the biggest barriers to achieving customer satisfaction in service delivery. No amount of training will enable your employees to serve customers well if your front-line people are inhibited by rigid policies and procedures. Your customers and potential customers will soon detect these barriers.

An example of where an employee exercised his prerogative and exceeded Tom's expectations occurred at a clothing store in the Mall of America. After buying some slacks, the salesman rang up the purchase. At the sales counter, Tom noticed some sampler bottles of cologne on sale for $7.50 and so he purchased one. But the salesman forgot to include the cologne in the purchase. As he handed Tom the credit card receipt to sign, he said, "Oh, I forgot to include your cologne." Then he added, "Oh, enjoy it; it's on me." While the cost of the sampler wasn't significant, it was obvious the salesperson didn't want to complicate the process by refiguring the sale, reproducing another credit card receipt, and causing Tom to wait five more minutes because of his oversight. So, the salesperson said, "enjoy it; it's on me." This is the kind of flexibility, trust, and empowerment we are encouraging you to give your employees.

▼ ASK YOUR CUSTOMERS IF YOUR TRAINING IS EFFECTIVE

We recently proposed a new approach to a client. While the idea of surveying their external customers to evaluate customer satisfaction was not new to the client, management felt the concept of asking those same customers to evaluate the company's training performance was innovative and refreshing. Their customers jumped at the chance to assess the company's technical and human skills competency.

They liked this approach because they realized that they would be the ultimate beneficiary from an improved quality service process. Who knows better than the customer what works and what doesn't? Even though the customer may not be aware of specific training programs, the customer can evaluate the end results—the company's quality and service delivery.

If your service delivery is effective, the customer usually will be satisfied. If the service delivery is lacking, you can trace back through the service delivery process and identify the problem areas. We believe that these are usually related to hiring and/or training at some employee job level, or to rigid policies.

When you ask your customers about the impact of your training, be sure to get background information about their functions and with whom they interact. Then determine the aspects of doing business with you which they like and those which could be improved. Find out if your people are knowledgeable, professional, and helpful, and whether they practice the "ABCDs of quality service"—do your people go "above and beyond the call of duty" for your customers?

Be sure to remember that your objective here is to learn the areas where you need to enhance your customer training process; it is not to focus on the malperformance of any employee nor is it to place blame, seek scapegoats, or intimidate your nonperformers. It is to determine if your training for front-line employees is effective.

Solicit feedback on ways you can improve your total quality process and overall service-delivery experience. Training is an important vehicle to help you get there.

▼ ACTING ON YOUR DATA

The information you gather from your employee and employee-related customer interviews will guide your action plans. The key to developing a successful program to help your employees be more effective is to be sure that it is relevant to the participants and that it is responsive to management's needs.

Always cultivate support among all levels of management. Regularly evaluate your processes and track the results so you can demonstrate your successes. However, the ultimate results will be found with your customers. Are they more satisfied with the quality of your service delivery or are they less satisfied? This is the "moment of truth" question we all must face.

▼ LARGE DOSES OF FORMAL INDIVIDUAL RECOGNITION AND TEAM REWARDS

We firmly believe that a company cannot overplay the impact of rewarding team effort and recognizing individual initiative, progress, and success. If there was but one wish we could magically grant every business, it would be the power to shower large doses of formal recognition on its people.

As companies come to terms with the importance of establishing formal and informal rewards and recognition programs for their employees and teams, there are a few guidelines we recommend.

1. *Give rewards and recognition to teams and individuals.*

2. *Make awards for individual effort, progress, and achievement;* however, do not let these awards overshadow or detract from any team

recognition. The psychology here is that everybody should be a team player. While lone rangers can make a big play, they seldom win Super Bowls. Instead, it's a team effort that usually wins the big game.

3. *Don't automatically appropriate cash for your awards.* We have found that a lunch or dinner where employees are recognized by a senior manager in their division can be of great value to employees. Teams who have worked effectively together frequently like to do things together. Tickets to a ball game or another event of their choice are often a good option.

We have also found that letting teams choose their own awards can be successful. A number of managers reject this idea outright. Some managers have told us they can't afford to let employees or teams select their own awards. Others have told us they'd lose control over their people. Still others have told us flat out that the practice of giving rewards is akin to paying people for what they're paid to do in the first place. We don't agree.

Our response to the reward "nay-sayers" is "What results do you desire from your people?" Do you want 70 percent effort from your people? How about 80 percent productivity? How about 95 percent goal achievement? Or would you be happy to exceed your departmental goals and corporate expectations by well over 100 percent? Rewards are paid for by the added performance of your people.

If you desire maximum results, then you must provide the maximum enticements for your people to achieve their goals. Behind this must be an acknowledgment that your employees are valued and can make a difference in the company.

In a total quality company, we believe an important reason for treating your employees with dignity and respect is so they will treat your customers the same way. That's it. We've seen both ends of the spectrum in many companies—those that achieve results because their employees are motivated and rewarded and those that don't achieve their desired results and do not reward or encourage their employees. But in those quality-driven and customer-focused companies that have achieved great results, we've seen the most motivated, energized, and also the most rewarded employees. If you had a choice, for which company would you rather work? We thought so!

One of those preferred companies is Federal Express. Janet Miller-Evans, a quality champion at Federal Express, told us, "In all my experiences, you can never give enough recognition."

Janet cited examples of recognition at Federal Express starting with the Bravo Zulu Award, an award whose name comes from the U.S. Navy's jargon for a *job well done.* A Federal Express manager can bestow a Bravo Zulu Award on the spot. It is given for clearly operating above and beyond one's job responsibilities. It can carry a monetary reward in the form of a check or a noncash reward such as a dinner or theater tickets. Then there is a Golden Falcon Award for recognition of service "above and beyond." Quality recognition for specific accomplishments is acknowledged by silver and gold pins which are given in conjunction with a meeting with Federal Express's CEO, Fred Smith. In addition to recognition through individual awards, Federal Express also honors teams through its Circle of Excellence Award, which is given monthly to top-performing groups.

Managers are empowered to set up their own departmental system of rewards and recognition. Janet said that in her department, which is East Central Region Sales, she has established a number of rewards to be given monthly, quarterly, and yearly for jobs well done. She showed us a list of the various types of awards for the East Central Region which were given out in 1992. This list and the accompanying descriptions covered an entire page. Given Federal Express's success, our feelings were reinforced that rewards—if well thought through—can never be "too much of a good thing."

At AT&T Universal Card Services Corp., a 1992 recipient of the Malcolm Baldrige National Quality Award, Rob Davis, Vice President and Chief Quality Officer, described to us how his company encourages outstanding service and employee performance. As previously noted, AT & T Universal Card Services (AT & T/UCS) is a relatively young company. It was established in March 1990. This has offered AT&T/UCS a unique opportunity to step away from the traditional, yet successful, management styles of its parent company and spread its wings in many unconventional ways. Davis told us that from the start, AT&T/UCS wanted its own identity and culture: "We believed that if we could premise our success on three statements, we could achieve our goals in a very short period of time." Those three guiding principles were:

1. An obsession with customer satisfaction.

2. Pleasing our associates.

3. Real focus on continuous improvement.

With these guiding objectives in place, AT&T/UCS set out to hire the very best people it could find. It adopted a clear customer satisfaction doctrine which translated into the best equipment, well-trained people, and an environment in which associates were rewarded for their suggestions and comments that led to significant improvements.

In many respects, these preconditions have set the stage for AT&T/UCS's rewards/recognition process. In fact, had AT&T/UCS not been so attentive to people at its inception, employees would not have been able to attain such outstanding results, according to Rob Davis.

▼ ENVIRONMENTAL REWARDS—THE PLACE WHERE WE WORK

Davis shared this example with us. "At AT&T/UCS, we look for ways to reward our people . . . one of our business objectives is to be the best at what we do. We have worked at making this facility a great place to work. Also, we take care of people's needs so they can take care of their customers. We have a fitness center which is open and staffed 24 hours a day. So, regardless of shifts or other pressing demands, our 2,600 employees and their spouses can utilize the fitness center."

Davis continued, "Rewarding people begins by giving our people a clear understanding of AT&T/UCS's vision and objectives so they know how they fit into the company's success." He added that the first day on the job, every employee goes through an orientation session that encompasses philosophy and values. These values as depicted in Figure 3-3 are also a puzzle that is part of the

Figure 3-3   AT&T Universal Card Services' Core Value

AT & T/UCS Rewards & Recognition Program. Associates award fellow associates with a puzzle piece when someone does something outstanding related to that core value.

In summary

- Recognize that management—through its words and actions—must demonstrate to employees that they are the company's greatest asset. Acknowledge the little things that people are doing right.
- Put an assessment process in place.
- Institute quality action teams and empower them to identify and implement improvements.
- Recognize that internal customers ultimately affect external results.
- Review employee job functions and track professional development.
- Eliminate or modify policies and procedures that affect customer satisfaction adversely.
- Recognize and reward employees. Rewards and recognition, if well thought through, can never be too much of a good thing.

CHAPTER FOUR

How to Evaluate Your Processes to Become More Customer-Focused

Think you can or think you can't and either way you'll be right.

HENRY FORD

Some time ago, we worked on a project involving robotics and the related software used in automating a manufacturing line. This is an area where we had no prior experience. Perhaps because of this, we found a number of surprises. Our first was that manufacturing can be very exciting when you view it as a process. Our second was a particularly important lesson.

We learned that the major improvements in converting to a more automated process did *not* come directly from the introduction of robotics and other automation. The key improvements were derived from carefully reviewing, understanding, streamlining, and then changing the process. When we reflected on this, we realized that this applies to most potential business improvements.

▼ FOCUS ON THE PROCESS

In his book *Business Process Improvement*, H. James Harrington says that "There is no product and/or service without a process and that likewise, there is no process without a product or service." He then states that in all companies there are hundreds of business processes going on every day and that over 80 percent of these are repetitive. When we think about this, we realize the vast opportunity for improvement.

"Customers today no longer take a microscopic view of your organization. There once was a time when you could build a good reputation by providing great products only. Today, however, customers view a potential supplier as a total entity. They expect every interface to be a pleasure."

To orchestrate these moments of truth, you must change your way of thinking, acting, and talking. You have to stop thinking about organizational structure and start focusing on the processes that control these interfaces," states Harrington. He illustrates this by juxtapositioning organizational ways of thinking against a process focus. We find his point of view not only thought provoking but also very much in line with our thinking on the importance of being both customer and process oriented. (See Table 4-1.)

Table 4-1 Corporate Points of View

Organizational Focus	*Process Focus*
Employees are the problem	The process is the problem
Employees	People
Doing my job	Help to get things done
Understanding my job	Knowing how my job fits into the total process
Measuring individuals	Measuring the process
Change the person	Change the process
Can find a better employee	Can improve the process
Motivate people	Remove barriers
Controlling employees	Developing people
Don't trust anyone	We are all in this together
Who made the error?	What allowed the error to occur?
Correct errors	Reducing variation
Bottom-line driven	Customer-driven

▼ DETERMINING YOUR BASELINE

Before you make changes, understand all relevant processes and measure all appropriate, countable elements of each process. This understanding and these measurements, which will be discussed in more detail later, provide the baselines against which improvements will be made.

Begin by carefully measuring and noting where you are today. This is your baseline.

Some examples of baseline number(s) are factors such as:

- Number of units processed.
- Number of steps in the process.
- Number of defects in the process.
- Length of time to complete a job.
- Customer rating of a particular factor on a numerical scale.

You may note that these factors are sometimes independent and sometimes interdependent. The improvement objective depends on the factor. Whenever it is appropriate, this specific objective should be meeting or exceeding customer expectations or exceeding current best-in-class performance.

Examples of improvements in this context are a *specified*:

- Increase in the number of units processed.
- Reduction in the number of steps in the process.
- Reduction of defects in the process.
- Reduction in the length of time to complete the job.
- Improvement in the customer satisfaction rating.

▼ AVOIDING THE "QUICK-FIX" SOLUTIONS

Always keep the effect on your customers in mind. Faster isn't better when it adversely affects quality. As you increase your response time, for example, be sure that the quality of your service does not deteriorate. When you "do it right," however, we have found that improved productivity and improved quality go hand in hand.

When you talked with your front-line employees as part of the background for your customer satisfaction measurement, it is likely that you identified roadblocks which inhibited getting things done effectively. Often, we have found that one of the biggest barriers to efficiency is that one department needs to wait for another department's input before proceeding. If the process is modified, it's often possible that these steps could be done in parallel, that one could be merged with the other, or even that one of the steps could be eliminated.

Discussions with your customers may have indicated not only areas of satisfaction and dissatisfaction, but also their source. You may have learned that a customer's delivery was delayed because of an incorrect address. In one case we encountered, this was due to the fact that address files simply weren't updated frequently enough.

In instances where your customers were dissatisfied, it is hoped that the problems have been fixed. But was the solution a Band-Aid™ or an interim solution? Since interim solutions solve problems readily, they have merit; however, if you resort to using too many of these "quick fixes," the system breaks down.

Another longer-term disadvantage of interim solutions is that they are often created outside of the normal process, which causes additional cumbersome work. This frequently takes place when an invoicing or billing system becomes obsolete. When this happens, software is written which is not integral to the entire process, making special manual efforts necessary to accommodate new products and new customer requirements.

This not only creates new possibilities for error, it can also create adverse effects on employee morale. Consequently, these patched processes should be among your first targets for goal setting and permanent improvement.

When an error occurs, make sure you understand at that point why it happened. This can enable the development of the long-term solution and, in some cases, prevent Band-Aid™ remedies.

Let's examine one example where it became evident that a long-term solution was identified as being necessary.

G. Fred DiBona, Jr., the energetic, take-charge CEO at Independence Blue Cross (IBC), headquartered in Philadelphia, discovered in the midst of revamping his customer service center that the current phone system was inadequate. Although DiBona was aware of IBC's high inbound call level and the fact that there had been customer complaints about their inability to reach the Blue Cross customer lines, he had not assessed the seriousness of the situation.

Rather than just add another line, however, DiBona and his staff made a thorough assessment of the situation. Through establishing measurement systems on how many calls were being put on hold, and for how long, and how frequently incoming calls received a busy signal, they realized that the time customers consumed in trying to reach IBC was significant. The problem was greater than they realized. Customers received a busy signal much too frequently. The customers' frustration, in turn, was felt by the IBC customer service representatives who had to bear the brunt of this customer frustration in the form of complaints, verbal indignities, and telephone hang-ups.

After identifying the nature of the problem and evaluating alternative solutions, IBC updated its telephone technology and capability and increased the number of inbound customer service representatives to handle peak call periods. These efforts substantially reduced the number of calls waiting as well as the busy signal counts. The good news for IBC now is better customer service as well as less stress and higher productivity among its front-line customer contact employees. Had IBC not conducted an assessment, chances are the magnitude of this problem would not have been detected before the impact resulted in a significant loss of customers or a diminished reputation.

▼ HOW TO FIND THE ROOT CAUSE OF A PROBLEM

In Masaaki Imai's book, *Kaizen*, he points out that often the first answer to a problem is not the root cause. Asking "why?" a number of times will identify several causes. This is much more likely to indicate the root cause. Imai cites the example of a former Toyota vice president, Taiichi Ohno's inquiry into the cause of a machine stoppage.

Question 1: *Why did the machine stop?*
Answer   1: *Because the fuse blew due to an overload.*

Question 2: *Why was there an overload?*
Answer   2: *Because the bearing lubrication was inadequate.*

Question 3: *Why was the lubrication inadequate?*
Answer   3: *Because the lubricating pump was not working right.*

Question 4: *Why wasn't the lubricating pump working right?*
Answer   4: *Because the pump axle was worn out.*

Question 5: *Why was it worn out?*
Answer   5: *Because sludge got in.*

Imai follows this by saying that, "By repeating 'why' five times, it was possible to identify the *real* cause and hence the *real* solution: attaching a strainer to the lubricating pump. If the workers had not gone through such repetitive questions, they might have settled with an intermediate countermeasure, such as replacing the fuse."

▼ IDENTIFY THE BEGINNING AND END OF THE PROCESS

When beginning to examine a process, be sure to start at the beginning. Although this may sound simplistic, there are a number of possible starting points; there is also potential for false closures in most processes.

An area where process is frequently examined is new product development and cycle time. It has been our experience that many people begin to measure the time to introduce a new service or product during the design phase or even at the time the design enters the development phase. *It needs to begin prior to that.*

Unless acceptance of viable new product proposals is a chronic stumbling block in your organization, we advise beginning the measurement of the cycle time when the idea to develop a product or service is accepted. "Accepted" means that *resources are applied to an idea to make it a program.* When your cycle time measurement begins after the true first phase of any process, you are kidding only yourselves.

Just as the beginning of cycle time measurement may be identified at too late a point in time, the end point is often a premature point. The net result is the same. The cycle time is viewed as being shorter than it actually is. In our example of the introduction of a product or service, the end point is sometimes seen as the point at which the product or service is first sold. The end point should be when there have been *successful* buyer transactions. If the service or product is not satisfactory and has to be adjusted, this must be factored in. (When this is the case, remember not only to analyze and correct the problem, but to document and change the process to prevent recurrence.)

▼ HOW TO CONDUCT A PROCESS EVALUATION

By conducting an in-depth process evaluation, you will be able to determine cycle time delays, opportunities for errors, and potential causes of employee and customer irritations.

Go to the source of the process and identify the starting point and hand-off points. You can then take notes about the process, what is dependent, independent, the sequence, and so on. This is especially important, but it can be tedious. There are alternatives, however. Today's technology is wonderful. A tape recorder can be a real asset here, or better yet, a video camera. In this way you can review and ensure that you haven't missed anything.

Document each step in the process. Note all factors. Unless you fully understand each step in the process and its relationship to the outcome, you won't know where the bottlenecks are, which steps can be shortened or eliminated, and, of course, how the process can be redefined.

As you proceed with a process evaluation, we suggest that you

- Determine the length of time to complete the entire transaction.
- Identify and count the number of steps involved.
- Measure the length of time in each step.
- Determine which steps are done sequentially and in parallel, and whether this procedure is appropriate.
- Note hand-off points—those places where the job is transferred to another person or function.
- Note critical decision points—where the next step is not automatic.
- Identify the number of possibilities for errors in each step of the process.
- Look at the possibility for bottlenecks both within each step and between steps, those places where the job does or could slow down.
- Determine which steps are not needed. (Are particular steps there "because they've always been there?").
- Examine people interaction and possibilities for error that could be removed or improved.
- Determine the costs of each step.
- Highlight the number of errors potentially visible to a customer.
- Examine customer satisfaction ratings and comments about factors which may be related to the process.
- Review the process in terms of its effects on customers, employees, and overall cost.
- Ask the people who do the work how they would improve the process.

When documenting a process, a commonly used tool is mapping or flowcharting. Designing a flow chart is aptly depicted as part of the training program, *First Class Service: The Training System for Continuous Quality Improvement*, published by Quality Resources. In this program they describe how to construct a flow chart by flowcharting the flowcharting process. We especially like this example and have included it as Figure 4-1.

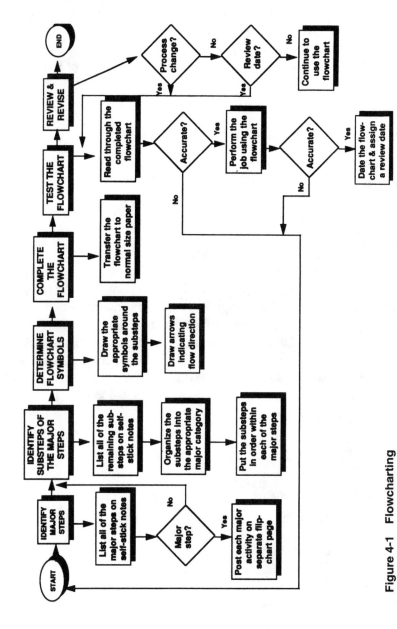

Figure 4-1 Flowcharting

Reprinted from *First Class Service: The Training System for Continuous Quality Improvement Workbook 1* © 1991 with permission of the publisher Quality Resources, White Plains, N.Y.

When you have developed a better understanding of your customers' requirements and have reviewed your processes, we'll wager that you have found some areas that need to be improved. How to proceed? We need to identify the causes. Then it is a matter of minding your P's and Q's.

- Qualify
- Quantify
- "Paretoize"
- Prioritize

▼ QUALIFY

To identify causes, we recommend brainstorming. If you have participated in a productive brainstorming session, you know that no idea is thrown out immediately. All thoughts are noted; sometimes these are then displayed on a large cause and effect diagram. This diagram, formerly known as the Ishikawa diagram, takes the shape of a fish. For this reason, it is more commonly known as a fishbone diagram or—relating to its purpose—a cause and effect diagram. When this technique is used, the bones stemming from the spine of the fish are labeled and causes are qualified by categories such as:

- Methods
- Materials
- Machinery or equipment
- Personnel or people

  Dependent on the use of the diagram, it can also include:

- Policies
- Procedures
- Environment, facility, or plant
- Quality

Thoughts are documented and grouped accordingly. After the brainstorming session, the ideas are then edited, combined, and regrouped as appropriate. We have found that the primary advantage to brainstorming is that ideas are thought starters which generate additional ideas. The cause and effect diagram is simply a tool which can be used to expedite problem solving.

There is a handy, minisized book called *The Memory Jogger, A Pocket Guide of Tools for Continuous Improvement,* distributed by Goal/QPC in Methuen, Massachusetts. It contains a number of examples of problem-solving tools, including examples of cause and effect diagrams.

In *The Memory Jogger,* the authors state that "a cause and effect diagram is used when you need to identify and explore and display the possible causes of a specific problem or condition." For every effect there are likely to be several major categories of causes which can be summarized under areas such as those we have specified. Although we typically work with widely used methods and materials any major category that emerges or helps people think creatively can be used.

Begin by placing the problem statement to the right, that is, in the head of the fish, and then place the brainstormed ideas in the appropriate major categories. For each cause ask, "Why does it happen?" List responses as branches of the major causes. (Remember: look to cure the cause and not the symptoms of the problem.) We have included an administrative service example of a cause and effect diagram from *The Memory Jogger* as shown Figure 4-2.

▼ QUANTIFY

When you begin to interpret, look for causes that appear repeatedly; gather data to determine the validity and relative frequencies of the different causes. We suggest that along the way you will also eliminate potential causes because they are not valid or are relatively insignificant.

110

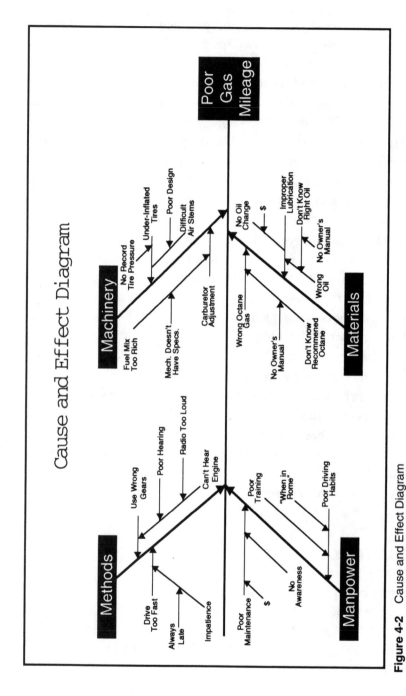

Figure 4-2 Cause and Effect Diagram

After grouping or clustering the causes or areas for improvement, quantify them; determine their degree of importance. Identify the most common cause, next most common, and so forth. These factors are often shown on a bar chart known as a Pareto diagram or chart. The term "paretoize" is our contrived derivation of that term.

▼ "PARETOIZE"/PRIORITIZE

In a Pareto diagram or chart, the categories are shown from left to right in their order of decreasing frequency; that is, the most common cause is shown as the tallest bar and is closest to the vertical axis. Other causes are then depicted in rank order of importance.

The Pareto diagram enables us to help determine the order in which we should solve problems. By "Paretoizing" and examining this chart, it is easy to see major areas for improvement, and the order and the magnitude of importance of each. Examples of Pareto charts from *The Memory Jogger* are shown in Figure 4-3. For additional information on Pareto diagrams and other charting techniques, see *SPC Simplified for Services: Practical Tools for Continuous Quality Improvement* by Amsden, Butler, and Amsden.

Let's return for a moment to *Kaizen*. We want to reemphasize the importance of identifying root causes. Keep investigating *why? why? why?* at the source of each problem. Fixing only the immediate cause is likely to solve only the current problem; it is unlikely to prevent recurrence.

Also, refer to the surveys of your employees' and customers' requirements. Once you have analyzed these and have evaluated each of the processes related to meeting those requirements, you will have identified ways to solve your customer-related problems. We are strong believers that ***the solution to a problem almost always emerges when you fully understand the problem.***

DIFFERENT USES OF A PARETO CHART

1) To identify the mot important problems through the use of different measurement scales, e.g., frequency, cost.
   Lesson: The most frequent problems are not always the most costly.

Field Service Customer Complaints:

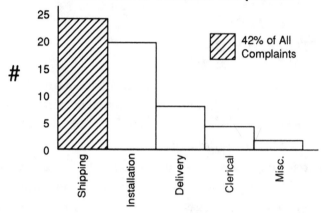

Cost To Rectify Field Service Complaints:

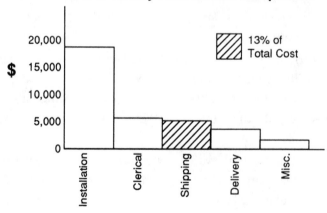

Figure 4-3   Different Uses of a Pareto Chart
Used with permission from *Memory Jogger: a Pocket Guide of Tools for Continuous Improvement,* © 1992 GOAL/QPC, 13 Branch Street, Methuen, MA 01844-1953.

2) To analyze different groupings of data, e.g., by product, by machine, by shift.
   Lesson: If clear differences don't emerge, regroup the data. Use your imagination.

Pareto Analysis Of The Number Of Defects

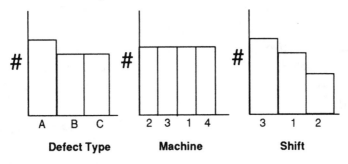

3) To measure the impact of changes made in a process, e.g., before and after comparisons.
   Lesson: You don't know how much better you are if you don't know where you were before the change.

Component Defects
(Station #2)

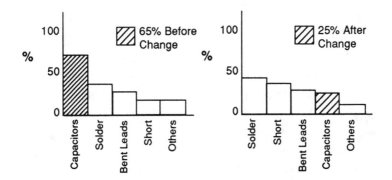

Figure 4-3 *continued*

Source: The Memory Jogger

▼ HOW TO GET THE IMPORTANT THINGS DONE FIRST

Earlier in this chapter we talked about priorities in relation to causes of problems. There is another aspect of priorities which is significant. This is in relation to managing time. One of the most knowledgeable people on this subject is Stephen Covey, author of *The 7 Habits of Highly Effective People.* We have used some of his concepts as the basis for our thinking.

In his book, Covey discusses setting priorities and managing time in order to accomplish goals. Dr. Covey suggests that we ask ourselves an important question: "What one thing could you do in your personal and professional life that, if you did it on a regular basis, would make a tremendous positive difference in your life?"

As a way of looking at priorities, Covey begins by identifying two factors that define activities; these are *urgent* and *important.* According to Covey, urgent means "it requires immediate attention. It's Now! *Urgent* things act on us."

A ringing telephone appears *urgent.* Covey adds that *urgent* matters are usually visible. They press on us; they insist on action. They're often popular with others. They're usually right in front of us. And often, they're pleasant, easy, fun to do. But so often they're *unimportant*!

Covey conveys that *importance,* on the other hand, has to do with results. If something is *important,* it contributes to your mission, your values, your high-priority goals. We react to urgent matters. But *important* matters that are not urgent require more initiative, more proactivity. We must act to seize opportunity to make things happen. If we don't have a clear idea of what is important, of the results we desire in our lives, we are easily diverted into responding to the *urgent.*

Covey shows these factors on a matrix which he has entitled *Time Management Matrix.* We have adapted Covey's matrix and call it *managing your priorities* as shown in Figure 4-4. View the *managing your priorities* matrix in terms of *managing time to accomplish meaningful results.* As you examine the matrix, ask yourself, "How do I spend my time?"

Each of the four quadrants depicts choices of areas on which we can spend time. According to Dr. Covey's teachings, quadrant 1 is both *Urgent* and *Important*. It deals with significant results that require immediate attention. These are often referred to as "crises" or "problems." But if we remain in quadrant 1 for too long, we experience stress, burnout, and crisis management syndrome and we develop a "firefighter" mind-set.

	Urgent	*Not Urgent*
Important	Quadrant 1 (Firefighter)	Quadrant 2 (Proactivator)
Not Important	Quadrant 3 (Short-Term Focuser)	Quadrant 4 (Decision-Escaper)

Figure 4-4   Managing Your Priorities

Source: Adapted from Stephen R. Covey, *The 7 Habits of Highly Effective People: Powerful Lessons in Personal Change.* Copyright © 1989 by Stephen R. Covey. Reprinted by permission of Simon & Schuster, Inc.

In quadrant 3, we deal with things that are *Not Important* but *Urgent*. This can include interruptions, meetings, and particularly, other people's agendas. According to Covey, people who spend most of their time in quadrant 3 have short-term focus and operate from a crisis management style. Their reputation takes on a chameleonlike character. They see goals and planning as worthless; yet they feel victimized by the system because they're not in control of the consequences. Finally, their relationships are shallow or broken. Needless to say, quadrant 3 is a pitiful state to be in.

Quadrant 4 is *Not Urgent* and *Not Important*. This is the quadrant most people escape to when overwhelmed and unable to confront reality or make decisions in their life—which is a decision in itself. Effective people, according to Dr. Covey, strongly avoid quadrants 4 and 3 because both areas result in a lack of accepting responsibility. It is the domain of people who limit their lives dealing with trivial matters.

Finally, there is quadrant 2. This, according to Stephen Covey, represents *Important* but *Not Urgent* issues. It is where the effective people dwell. Covey says, "It is the heart of effective personal management. It deals with things that are not urgent, but they are important. It deals with things like building relationships, writing a personal mission statement, engaging in long-range planning, exercising, preventive maintenance, preparation—all those things we need to do, but somehow seldom get around to doing because they aren't urgent."

We encourage you to examine the priorities that will make the biggest difference to your customers and employees. Ask yourself, "What needs to be done in my organization?" Then devote your time to those issues and ensure that your staff devotes its time to these priorities. Excellent performance does not happen by accident.

In summary

- Begin thinking and planning from a process focus rather than an organizational focus.
- Determine your baselines by understanding and measuring all appropriate elements of each process.
- Avoid "quick-fix" solutions whenever possible.
- Find the root cause of problems.
- Be sure you correctly identify the beginning and end of the process.
- Take advantage of analysis tools and techniques.
- Get the important things done first.

CHAPTER FIVE

How to Benchmark and Set Customer-Focused Goals

I hear you say "Why?" Always "Why?" You see things and you say "Why?" But I dream things that never were, and I say "Why not?"

GEORGE BERNARD SHAW

▼ BENCHMARKING

Webster's dictionary defines bench mark (two words) as "a point of reference for making measurement." From a business perspective, we like the simplicity of the definition used by Corning, Inc. Corning defines benchmarking (one word) as "the process of rigorously comparing parts or all of a product, service, or function against the best in the marketplace."

We also like another definition, used by the Government Systems & Technology Group in Motorola, because of its specificity:

Benchmarking is the continuous process of:

- Determining critical success factors, those factors that are critical to the long-term success of your department.

- Comparing your own performance on the factors to your toughest competitors or best-in-class performers.

- Using the information to develop business strategies, functional action plans and standards of performance.

The goal of benchmarking which accompanies this Motorola-based definition "is to exceed the best competitor or best-in-class company in the critical success factors relevant to the strategy of each business unit."

What are some of these critical success factors? Why benchmark? A friend of ours, Allan Juers, a vice president of Towers Perrin, suggests some possible reasons when he talks about benchmarking:

How can we ensure our costs are competitive?

Do we really need this many people to perform this function?

How can we upgrade the quality of our products?

What should we set as targets for productivity improvements?

How should we resolve _____ (fill in your organization's most intractable problem).

Allan and his colleagues at Towers Perrin categorize types of benchmarking into strategic, organizational, and operational. This made perfect sense to us when Allan talked about it; we realized, however, that we had not previously thought about this categorization in terms of understanding improvement opportunities. Figure 5-1 can help you to correlate your specific needs with the definition and purpose of those needs.

It seems like only yesterday; yet it seems like 50 years ago when we consider how modern business practices have changed since that time. In reality, it was about 15 years ago when we first became involved in a complex benchmarking project, probably one of the first efforts of this type. Although now referred to as benchmarking, that term, in this context, was then unknown.

When we began this project, it was part of a competitive analysis process at Xerox. To achieve our objectives, we looked first at Xerox's products and product costs. Then we dismantled imported equipment; we costed every part and then estimated overheads, labor, and so on. We made an educated guess (in yen) of the competitive products' costs and compared and recalculated these against our own "equivalent" dollar figure for every possible element.

Type	Definition	Level of Organization	Purpose of Benchmarking
Strategic	• Broad measures of financial market position • Key elements of strategy	• Company, business unit, or division	• Supplement or test strategic plans
Organizational	• Staffing levels • Staffing mix • Structure • Costs	• Department or function	• Control or reduce costs • Reallocate resources
Operational	• Tactics and approaches for key functions and processes • Performance levels • Costs	• All levels	• Enhance quality and effectiveness of functions and processes • Control or reduce costs

Figure 5-1 Types of Benchmark Measures
Source: Allan Juers, Towers Perrin, Chicago, Illinois

The intent of our Xerox benchmarking effort was sincere and the dedication noteworthy, but we did a lot of things wrong, some of which we recognized and tried unsuccessfully to escalate at the time. Some other potential weaknesses did not surface until later.

As we reconstruct what happened, we realize that we really didn't understand all our own numbers, plus we badly miscalculated our competition for a lot of reasons. An example was that we couldn't comprehend the value of "not reinventing the wheel" with each product we produced. We valued creativity to a fault. We totally changed designs and part specifications with each product that we made.

In contrast, the Japanese understood that using a tried and tested part meant not only cost reduction due to volume production, but also an *assurance of reliability*. During that time, Xerox, and most other large American manufacturers, purchased from a great many suppliers who had varying degrees of product consistency and reliability. We didn't even know about, let alone understand, supplier partnerships.

But our worst judgment was beyond these factors. It was that we, who had been best-in-class, stopped leading the way. The most critical error was that Xerox, which had set the standard, began to set goals based on its emerging competitors' standards. That, in itself, was a problem. To compound this, goals were set based on where competitors were that day, not where they would be next year and the year after that.

As a result of not looking forward, and not recognizing the needs of its customers and its own strengths, Xerox lost significant market share. The good news is that Xerox has regained share and is recognized today as one of the leaders in both the benchmarking process and in supplier relationships. In fact, one of the earliest and still one of the best examples of positive results of benchmarking is Xerox's change of its order processing procedures based on a benchmarking effort outside the office equipment industry. In order to streamline its process dramatically, Xerox benchmarked L. L. Bean's excellent order processing activity and then tailored it to meet Xerox requirements.

A more recent example of a successful benchmarking effort, one in which both Xerox and L. L. Bean were among the "benchmarked" companies, was conducted by Delta Dental Plan of Massachusetts. The Delta Dental Plan of Massachusetts' total quality management program was a winner of the Coopers & Lybrand/*Sloan Management Review* Quality Award. Delta's quality program is described by Thomas Raffio, Senior Vice President of Operations, in the Fall 1992 issue of the *Sloan Management Review*.

In this article, Raffio describes the importance of benchmarking as a key to Delta's improvement process. One of the areas which they benchmarked was customer service. The cross-functional committee responsible for the benchmarking effort at Delta chose companies which were "the best of the best" in or outside the insurance industry, were Malcolm Baldrige winners or finalists, had "one-stop" shopping for their customers, or had guaranteed service levels.

According to Raffio, the committee chose the following performance measures:

- Absentee rate of customer service associates

- Turnover

- Internal promotions

- Overtime

- Training time

- Management (i.e., whether customer service is managed by Marketing or Operations)

- Type and timeliness of information to marketing

- Call volume per customer service associate

- Percentage of callers abandoning

- Percentage of calls answered by a customer service associate within 10 seconds

- Information callbacks

- Average time per call

The committee "used information from this benchmarking to redesign the customer service department to maximize efficiency, improve external service and minimize employee stress. The redesign involved purchasing and installing a new Automatic Call Distributor (ACD); redesigning job functions to emphasize team servicing; changing layout of furniture and equipment to support job redesign; training all customer service team members; implementing computerized tools for categorizing calls, interpreting and addressing reasons for calls, and facilitating correspondence turnaround."

This new system automatically provides a number of statistics which were not previously available or had to be calculated manually. Having these kinds of numbers is important to monitoring and maintaining high levels of quality.

Raffio stated that the results have been dramatic. Even before the new phone system had been installed, the percentage of calls answered by customer service associates within 10 seconds had improved by over 100 percent without adding staff and with no employee turnover.

Since our initial benchmarking at Xerox, we have been involved in many benchmarking efforts, which, like Delta's, have resulted in significant improvements. Based on our experiences, we have developed a process that works for us. It's really quite simple, but like many successful efforts, its success is dependent on a carefully thought-out objective and a thorough understanding of your own processes before proceeding. The importance of this initial work, which is critical to the success of benchmarking, is often overlooked or not included because of the time involved.

Before we introduce the steps of the process which we have found works well, we'd like to share an example of a company which followed most of these steps in trying to learn how to improve its return on capital. Since this company did not wish to be identified, we will call it IMI.

IMI, a large diversified company, was facing severe competition and as a result had lowered its prices and was earning a return on capital employed that was far below its cost of capital. The management team chosen to evaluate this identified several core activities that needed major reengineering to become more efficient and cost-effective. Breakthrough thinking was needed. Cross-functional teams were then assigned to the project.

The team dealing with logistics and marketing/distribution activity was made up of:

> The head of the centralized order entry and dispatch.
>
> The manager of the largest terminal.

The shift supervisor of the terminal.

The purchasing agent for raw materials.

The plant planning manager.

The marketing manager for several product lines.

The first task was to establish a team objective or charter. This objective was:

To develop improved processes for the planning, scheduling, and management of the product supply and distribution system to deliver to customers more quickly and reliably at the most economic level.

The team then developed a flow chart depicting the very complex distribution network from the company's plants to customers. This chart was the framework for charting the information flow and decision points that were involved in managing the distribution system. The organization was also examined to determine the "who and how" of the various forecasts, negotiations, and decisions that were involved.

It took the team quite a while to unravel how the system really operated, and a number of interviews were needed to validate and then correct misconceptions about how certain reports were used, the source of sales forecasts, who made specific decisions, and so on. It turned out that no one below the president was responsible for inventory-level management because of the fragmented, compartmentalized organization. Numerous other problems were identified through flow charting:

- Inconsistent and inaccurate forecasts
- No mechanism for auditing the accuracy of estimates and entering the results into next month's forecast
- Time-consuming and manpower-intensive coordination of product supply and demand
- Ineffective use of centralized supply support

- Use of two different product and scheduling systems with parallel functions and similar data requirements that had not been linked to a common database

- Varying schedules

- Inconsistent or incomplete reporting

The next step was to ask customers to evaluate the distribution system of their suppliers. Questions were asked about IMI's distribution performance to help identify the categories for subsequent benchmarking.

The team then benchmarked best-in-class companies. When the benchmarking was completed, the team said that this step was invaluable in providing insight into what was achievable. Perhaps more important, it gave the team confidence that significant improvement could be realized by IMI.

Some of the lessons learned through the benchmarking are shown in Table 5-1.

Table 5-1 Lessons Learned from Benchmarking

Lesson	Type of Company
Configuration of a lean, flat organization with clean lines of responsibility and authority at the appropriate level	Chemical companies Independent trucking firm
Effective use of computer systems	Regional retailer Biscuit producer

Use of timely accurate information
  Performance feedback
  Single set of forecasts
	Paper manufacturer

Benchmarking best practices together with the collective thoughts of team members and recommendations made by others during the validation process were used as the framework for developing the model for improvement.

At an early stage, the team began to focus on the need for major structural changes to achieve the desired improvements. In particular, it was concluded that a structure was required which provided clear, unified accountability for the supply and distribution of all products to the customer.

In identifying the best solution, the team considered

- The need to provide a single, best forecast of product demand that was clearly linked to the profit plan and business strategies.

- The need for greater focus on the customer.

- The need to put responsibilities for major business activities in the right place.

- The development of a structure that had fewer levels and broader spans of control and was better integrated.

- The need to make better use of existing systems and enhance ownership/responsibility for data input.

- The need to make a major break with the existing structure and culture.

As required by the team's objective, the recommended changes improved the planning and scheduling and management processes. It accomplished this by eliminating several functional boundaries and consequent interface problems. It also reduced two to three levels of management supervision. Analysis which had been carried out by three functions was coordinated into a single group. Similarly, scheduling and shipping operations were restructured to eliminate redundancy and conflicting information.

The new model enhanced customer focus by establishing a tight link between order taking and delivery scheduling and the management of the truck fleet operation.

After these changes were implemented by IMI, there was significant performance improvement. In retrospect, it was the benchmarking experience, that is, seeing what was possible and understanding how other companies achieved superior results that gave IMI the courage to make major changes in such a core business activity.

There are many companies that, like IMI, have benefited significantly by benchmarking others and learning what is possible to achieve improved performance. As a result of looking at companies like IMI and how they benchmarked successfully, we have developed a process which you may want to use as a reference for your benchmarking efforts. A description of this process follows. This is summarized in Figure 5-2.

Step 1: Establish objective. Schedule an initial meeting of the appropriate people to determine what you want to accomplish; record the overall objective and preliminary subobjectives and review them. Schedule a subsequent meeting or meetings to agree on the "final" objectives and determine the roles of those present and any others who should be part of the benchmarking effort.

Step 2: Map and evaluate your company's processes as related to your objective. Because understanding your processes prior to benchmarking others is an absolute must, we encourage you to make sure that you map your processes as described in Chapter 4 prior to proceeding. Quantify as many areas as you can; for example, how long does it take to process an order; within that time frame, how much time is spent on each activity. The information may not be perfect, but it will represent approximate baselines to compare with respondents' answers.

Make sure that all participants who are involved in your benchmarking project understand your own processes. Without a thorough understanding of where you are today, you will obtain answers which may not be relevant. More important, when you evaluate your interview findings, you will realize that you have a long list of questions that you did not ask.

Step 3: After you have evaluated your processes, determine drivers for improvement. At this juncture, stop and look at what you want to improve. When you go out to search for answers, what are the critical

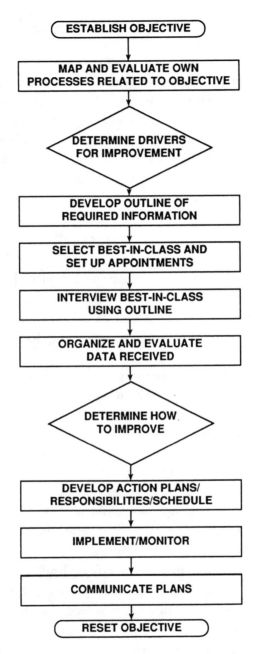

Figure 5-2 Benchmarking Process

factors that you seek to change? The team of people addressing this issue should agree on these factors.

Step 4: Document your specific objectives (your expected deliverables) in an outline of required information. Document your expected deliverables. Unless you do this, you won't cover all bases, and you are likely to talk to one company about certain aspects of the process and another about other aspects. As a result, you won't be able to combine what you have learned. This is especially important if various people involved in the benchmarking effort conduct interviews at different companies.

Documenting your objectives helps you to be consistent in your pursuit of knowledge. However, it is also important to be flexible. The topics don't have to be addressed in a specific order; let the conversation flow. Additionally, you may have forgotten to include a particular topic; let the respondents lead you to subjects you may not have pursued. Remember the importance of listening closely.

Step 5: Select the best-in-class companies in terms of the factors you want to improve and set up appointments for personal or in-depth telephone interviews. Firms that are best-in-class in a specific discipline can be identified in a number of ways. These can range from a hotel you always prefer because of their service to a credit company or a bank you choose because of the accuracy of their statements. Your own personal and professional experiences may be valid indicators of an excellent process. These companies do not need to be "superstars" in all areas, but they should be significantly better than your firm in the particular dimension you wish to improve.

A more common method of identifying leading-edge companies is through speakers at conferences geared to the subject you want to benchmark. Attendees at these conferences can also be excellent sources; we have found that networking at these forums can be of great value. Professional associations, user groups, your suppliers, and trade publications can also be important leads.

Remember to minimize the time you require when you set up and conduct interviews; the people from whom you are requesting help are likely to have to compensate your interview time with their own personal time. Some information will be confidential; do not ask questions that you would not answer for your own company. Pretest your outline on one of the divisions of your company and/or at a firm where a friend works. Whenever possible, offer to share expertise in an area where your company excels, or, if appropriate, share your interview findings.

Step 6: Interview those you have identified following the outline you have developed. As you interview people, keep your drivers for improvement and your own processes at the forefront of your mind. When you hear something that may be important, stop, think, and listen to the answers in terms of your processes. When you understand your own processes, you will see the "Aha's," that is, the potential fixes for the areas in which you have identified weaknesses.

Step 7: Organize and evaluate the data you gather. One thing we preach but don't always practice is to debrief with others on our team or at least rewrite our own notes *immediately*. When we don't do this, we are always sorry. Somehow, a week later, when we read our notes, there are always thoughts which are not clear. As you begin to organize and evaluate your data, look for similarities of excellence among processes of the companies you have interviewed; determine if these are applicable to your processes.

Step 8: Determine how to improve. Be sure to tie this back to your objective. This is the start of the implementation process. Now that you have assimilated your information, look again at your objectives and superimpose this new knowledge onto your objectives. If you mapped your own processes at the outset and asked the appropriate questions based on your drivers for improvement, you should have a number of valuable answers to improving the quality of your processes.

Step 9: Develop action plans/responsibilities, budget plans, and schedules. None of this is really worthwhile unless it initiates change. To affect timely change, it is necessary to develop specific action plans. Determine these plans, set names against them based on function and expertise, and then put dates in place to enable tracking. Putting dates against these plans will help ensure timely deployment. However, it should be remembered that the time involved may be over and above the normal job function of the people to whom these actions are assigned.

Implementation may also require incremental resources—additional dollars and people. When this is the case, development of a proposal with costs and benefits will be required. The benefits are likely to more than balance the costs, but it is possible that this will have to be demonstrated and sold to other departments and functions and a higher level of management.

Step 10: Implement plans and monitor performance. Once each person carries out her or his responsibilities and the appropriate people have been sold on the recommended changes, the overall implementation of improving the quality of a process or processes can be put in place. To ensure an effective implementation and to identify possible areas for further improvement, the changed processes should be remapped and monitored on a regular basis. The schedule for this is highly dependent on the kind of process, its inherent volatility, and its effect on competition.

Step 11: Communicate plans. The best of improvements can be unraveled by not communicating the changes to others who may be affected. Often, quality improvements reduce cycle time significantly. If those who receive the output are not alerted to this, *that* time reduction and, possibly even more time, could be lost. (Note that, in some cases, this communication may be critical prior to implementation and should take place in step 9 or earlier.)

Step 12: Reset objectives. Just when you thought you were done, it may be time to start all over again.

Additional Important Notes on Benchmarking

Our suggested process differs from most others in its strong emphasis on upfront planning and the understanding of your own processes at the outset. We also emphasize the importance of communications and the effect that your changes could have if they are not communicated adequately. There are some other important elements which are sometimes overlooked that we would like to emphasize.

Understand That Others Move Forward

Perhaps this sounds like a given. However, remember that we missed it altogether when we did our initial benchmarking. Even today, it is sometimes not addressed in the implementation of improvements based on benchmarking. To take full advantage of benchmarking and to become or remain leading edge, you need to forecast where others will be and exceed that target.

Emphasize Your Strengths

When you begin talking with other companies, you are likely to see areas where you are strong. Applaud yourselves. Leverage these advantages. Let your customers know. And keep improving.

Document and Adhere to Your Objectives Unless the Environment Changes Substantially

When you know where you are going, you can lead with strength; don't veer from your course easily, but don't resist changing if there is a more positive course.

Be Consistent, Yet Flexible, in Your Pursuit of Knowledge

Old truths can abide or they can tarnish with age; balance tested wisdom with acceptance of new ideas.

▼ REALISTIC GOALS AND REACHOUT GOALS

There are two schools of thought on goal setting. The first has become almost a cliche, that is, setting *realistic goals;* the second is setting *reachout goals.* We once felt that we had to choose one or the other. Now, we believe they should coexist.

We need realistic goals—those goals which seem within reach—to accomplish short-term improvements. However, these "reachable" goals alone are not likely to produce outstanding achievements. The highest level of accomplishment requires a reachout goal—a goal that requires a major change in the way in which something is accomplished.

To integrate reachout goals and realistic goals, we recommend making realistic goals the tactical subsets of reachout goals.

George Fisher, Chairman and Chief Executive Officer of Motorola, talks about the importance of reachout goals, striving for a 10 times or 100 times improvement rather than a 10 percent improvement. If you say that you will improve 10 percent, you'll probably do just that—improve 10 percent. You will whittle away at the process and make minor adjustments here and there and, eventually, reach your 10 percent goal. But, to achieve a 10-fold or 100-fold improvement, you have to change the process. George's point is that you have to *change the process* to achieve significant improvement.

Motorola began setting reachout goals in 1981 when senior management decided that Motorola's product quality was not good enough. At that time a goal was set which appeared to be impossible to meet—a tenfold improvement in quality in *five* years. This goal was accomplished, in part, by accompanying it with some important changes in priorities. One example of this was that instead of financial measurements being the first topic on the agenda of Operating and Policy Committee meetings, quality measurements became the first topic of discussion. This continues to be the case today at Motorola.

After achieving, on average, the first ten times improvement goal, Motorola discovered, *not* that the goal was impossible, but that it was not ambitious enough. At the beginning of 1987, a new quality goal was set which was to achieve at least a 100-fold improvement by 1991. In mid-1993, Motorola could point proudly to a 170-fold improvement that it had made in reducing in-process defects and improving the overall quality level of its products.

If you set realistic goals only, you are shortchanging yourself and/or your organization. *Don't confine your goal setting to "realistic" goals.*

Easy, not at all! But it is possible! And, if you don't do it, someone else will, possibly a company which doesn't understand the old process and is not inhibited by it. Very often the most important innovations are made by a new company (or an old company entering a new business) because new companies are not tied to the "This is the way we've always done it" mentality.

Although new entries into a business will probably continue to be the most innovative, this does not always have to be the case. Imagine having the expertise in a business, but also being able to make major changes. Talk about having the edge! You've got it!

A place where they were not tied to "This is the way we've always done it" but has successfully blended tradition with the future is the Del Mar Thoroughbred Club near San Diego, California. Under the direction of Joseph Harper, Del Mar has been brought to the forefront of thoroughbred racing and also is known as a site for special events in a highly competitive Southern California community.

As Harper tells the story, he realized that people would come to San Diego as long as the sun shined. But he also realized that Del Mar could not remain just a racetrack. It had to become a destination—a special event in itself—that could compete with the likes of Disneyland, Sea World, the San Diego Zoo, and the Wild Animal Park. And, of course, with year-round temperatures in the 70s, a day at the beach or the ball game is often an option for locals and for tourists.

Harper's Del Mar "reachout" goal was to transform aging grandstands and grounds into a first-class facility that both horsemen and patrons would want to visit on a repeated basis. Harper says that what makes Del Mar unique is its people and the personality of the track. "The track has a personality all its own and a glorious history," Harper told us. But he is constantly aware that it also has a future and it is up to the people to keep that personality and history alive.

At the start of the 1991 racing season, Harper told his employees, "In the next three years, we will build the finest race track in the world.

But only half of that will be built with brick and mortar. The other half—the most important half—is the human side. This is what you and I will build together. By sharing the enthusiasm, excitement, and expectations we have for this place, a new Del Mar will emerge, an organization that will continue to be simply the best in the business."

Harper's long-range strategy for accomplishing his goal was four-fold. With the strong support and encouragement of Del Mar's Board Chairman, John C. Mabee, Harper set out to modernize Del Mar as the preeminent racetrack in the nation. Second, he increased the racetrack's visibility by offering a high-stakes, million-dollar race. This gave birth to the Pacific Classic, which was introduced in 1991. Third, legislation was passed that allowed Del Mar to participate in the intertrack wagering system which permits off-track crowds to wager on Del Mar races at 13 satellite betting sites. Finally, and very important, Harper put into motion a plan to upgrade the professionalism and customer relations skills of his employees. This is no simple feat considering that the work force population of the Del Mar racetrack swells from 50 to 1,700 employees during its six-week racing season.

Just before the racing season officially starts, these seasonal employees begin to arrive at Del Mar. What could have the makings for a major disaster in scheduling and human resource management typically goes off without a hitch due to Del Mar's attention to detail and the longevity of so many of Del Mar's seasonal employees. Opening day at the races strikes one as much of a class reunion as it does the kick-off of a multimillion-dollar seasonal business.

Since 1989, Del Mar has been the number one rated racetrack in North America as measured by the amount of money bet on its races. It has achieved all four of its goals with the reconstruction of the grandstands, including a new 14,300-seat, $80 million structure. The improvements at Del Mar to date have not only protected its customer base, but have attracted new patrons, thus increasing their business significantly.

Setting and achieving goals can generate improvements in productivity, in revenues, and in the quality of products and services; these, in turn, can produce substantial cost savings.

Because goals, particularly reachout goals, can be widespread in their intent and potential impact, they need to be linked to your firm's fundamental objectives. Without this linkage and selling of the importance of these goals at all levels, the "nay-sayers" will win out. When you're striving for a reachout goal of a 10-fold or a 100-fold improvement, most people can be easily convinced that it can't happen. And, change can't happen, unless people believe it can happen!

If a goal's sponsorship is from the top and pervasive throughout and people within the organization have a positive, "We can do it" attitude, the sky is the limit. To achieve the greatest gains, reorganizations may be necessary. This includes changing provincial boundaries so that turf protection is put out of its traditional balance, allowing players to think more broadly.

Where do you find solutions that will enable you to think more broadly? As a start to changing the paradigm, look outside your industry, outside your function for clues to a different process.

We mentioned earlier that when Xerox decided it needed to streamline and cut the costs of its order process, it looked to L. L. Bean, which clearly couldn't be profitable if it had order costs as high as Xerox's at that time.

At Milliken, Bob Anderson couldn't find a marketing model that met his needs. Instead of giving up or "starting from scratch," he converted a friend's medical diagnostics model to a marketing tool. Through some clever reprogramming and tailoring to fit his need, he gained an asset which his competitors didn't have. When you look outside your industry for answers, the answers aren't likely to be a glovelike fit. You will need to make changes like modifying software as Bob did.

Or if your company is a manufacturing firm, and service is peripheral to your business, you may want to look at firms where service is their business. This can provide you with ways of doing things differently. The secret to looking beyond your usual horizon is that you will begin to think differently. Even if you don't find the specific solution in your search, you will have begun to approach the problem from a different perspective.

Before you begin to set specific goals, understand the processes and measure all relevant, countable elements of each process as described in Chapter 4. This understanding and these measurements provide the baselines against which improvements will be made.

If you need to improve a process, look at your best competitor and the best-in-class anywhere. When you use the performances of the best in determining your goal, don't ever forget that the best won't be standing still. By the time you reach your goal, it is likely that the best will have exceeded their past record.

As a basis for your goals, whenever it is relevant, your customers' and your potential customers' expectations should be your *minimum* goal. Where your company is an industry leader, your goals should be to set new standards in that industry.

One company that sets its goals based on understanding its customers' needs is K-Swiss, Inc., one of America's leading manufacturers of athletic footwear. K-Swiss understands customers' requirements, in part, through its being a different kind of supplier. It works directly with retailers and customers, making sure that K-Swiss manufactures the kind of shoe that customers want for each of their athletic needs. Then, it trains its retailers to understand and talk with customers about these value-added features.

Steven Nichols, the President of K-Swiss, told us that K-Swiss, in its early years, withdrew from its largest retailer because that retailer was unwilling to take time for training to understand customers' requirements and to sell to these requirements. As he explained to us, "We want our shoes to be sold by people who understand fit and the use of shoes for the sport for which they were designed. If you wear a basketball shoe and play tennis," he said, "you will wear out the toe. Tennis shoes have extra rubber in the toes because tennis players drag their toes, which basketball players don't do."

K-Swiss constantly improves its products. Instead of reacting to fashion trends, it refines its basic products based on feedback on features such as height and padding. As a result, K-Swiss believes that it achieves standards of much better fit and longer wear.

K-Swiss's product improvements are based primarily on constant interaction with its customers and retailers and in-depth customer research, which includes obtaining a thorough understanding of customers' requirements. This provides a sound foundation for making product improvements.

Under some circumstances, interviews to supplement your customer satisfaction research will be required. For example, if you are interested in your customers' acceptance to a change in your system or their views about a proposed new product or service, you will need to test your customers' specific reactions to that proposal. The customer, in this case, could be not only the buyers of your products or services, but it could be an internal department, a reseller, a service provider, or a supplier.

There are a number of instances when your "customers" could be your suppliers. For example, if you are planning electronic transmission of data to suppliers' locations, you will need to obtain a thorough understanding of their requirements.

▼ SETTING GOALS BASED ON CUSTOMERS' EXPECTATIONS

When you use customer expectations as the basis for your goals, review the research data. To determine the course for improvement, analyze all available information specifically related to a problem.

As an example, assume that the predominate customer satisfaction rating for your sales responsiveness has been a "3" on a five-point scale, with "5" being very satisfied. A possible goal could be that at least 90 percent of your customers rate the service response time of your firm as a "4" or "5" within one year.

Let's assume that the customer research data show that dissatisfaction with response time is due to sales representatives' not returning calls promptly.

Our customers' expectations are within three business hours, but many of our sales representatives are returning calls the next business day or in six to eight business hours. Evaluation of the process indicates that our salespeople are not able to retrieve messages readily from the field.

We have already accomplished three important presteps prior to setting our goal.

1. We have done thorough research to identify the specific area of dissatisfaction.

2. We understand our customers' expectations.

3. We know our current level of performance.

Let's set a goal. The goal is that our sales representatives respond to every customer call within three business hours and that all the appropriate systems are in place to allow this to happen.

Steps toward achieving the goal are

- Assign responsibility for verifying the root cause of the problem.
- Benchmark several best-in-class companies to determine their standards and techniques for achievement.
- Arrange meeting(s) among all affected departments. (This might be message center support, telecommunications, administration, and sales.)
- Determine actions and prepare an action plan with assigned responsibility by department.
- Determine schedule and set specific targets and due dates for implementing solutions. (In turn, each affected department will need to assign specific responsibilities and interim dates.)
- Arrange for and provide any necessary equipment and training.
- Communicate the plan.
- Implement the plan.
- Monitor to ensure achievement and adherence.
- Reward achievement.

- If best-in-class performance is better than goal, set new higher goal.

To ensure that your goals are achieved,

- Be sure that there is buy-in through involvement of all the appropriate people.
- Make sure that communications are clear, positive, and directed to all who will be impacted.
- Review organizational structures and make changes which may be required for effective implementation.
- Develop baseline numbers using current measurements.
- Have the people who work the process help in determining how to improve it.
- Plan for effects on employees, suppliers, and customers.
- Set intermediate goals and deadlines.
- Designate specific responsibility, authority, and resources to achieve goals.
- Set achievement targets and dates.
- Positively support all accomplishments.
- Celebrate success.
- Monitor and report on a frequent, regular schedule.
- Reward excellence.

When the improvements are made, no matter how great, they will be viewed as change. People have problems with change even when it is a positive move. Effective communications can do a lot to overcome this.

Also, we have found that when those who will be most affected by the change have been planners for the change, they will make it happen. Otherwise, these employees may reluctantly "go along with the change" or worse yet, try to sabotage it.

The firms that will make the greatest future progress will be those whose leaders inspire their employees to make significant improvements, provide them with the knowledge and resources to move forward, and recognize and reward their achievements.

In summary

- Ensure that you understand your own processes thoroughly before benchmarking others.

- Set objectives and outline what you wish to accomplish through the benchmarking process prior to proceeding.

- Identify companies which are superior to your company in the particular process which you want to improve; very often, they do not have to be in the same or even a related industry.

- Recognize that benchmarking is worthwhile only if you carefully evaluate your findings and take actions for improvement based on tailoring what you learned to fit your objectives.

- Set reachout goals—goals that require you to change the process in order to meet them.

- Measure, monitor, communicate, and reward at every appropriate opportunity.

CHAPTER SIX

How to Educate and Train Your Employees in the Ways of Excellent Customer Service

*Americans still care about quality. The country is full of
intelligent, courageous people who would change if they
only knew how.*

DR. W. EDWARDS DEMING

Education and training is a lifelong journey. In the past 10 years,
American-based companies have invested more in the education and
training of their employees than in the previous 100 years combined.
At the same time, America's international competitors also are increasing budgets to further the training and professional development of their employees.

Regrettably, however, there are still too many businesses which
have been slow to invest improvements for long-term success, and
thus these companies lag behind their competition in terms of quality and customer satisfaction. In the 1970s and 1980s, while foreign
corporations were spending huge sums to modernize their factories
and train their employees in innovative quality techniques (albeit
with the support of their national governments), many American
corporate leaders were distracted by mergers, leveraged buyouts,
and manufacturing products in aging factories, often with outmoded equipment. As a result, these American products often failed
to meet customers' needs.

145

In the late 1980s, corporate America began to awake from two decades of benign neglect to its customers and realized that—as a nation and economic power—we were losing our clout in the global marketplace. CEOs like Donald Petersen of Ford Motor Company began to instigate change. Petersen, in his book, *A Better Idea*, describes how he became a convert of W. Edwards Deming, the father of Japanese quality methods, and championed a quality initiative process that ultimately restored Ford Motor Company briefly as the top-ranked U.S. automobile manufacturer. If you consider the tremendous sales and marketing advantage General Motors enjoyed over Ford at the time, this achievement of replacing GM at the top, even for a brief period, was an amazing feat. Even more amazing, it was accomplished primarily by training and educating employees in basic quality processes.

But how? Petersen says one key was to involve Ford's employees in all phases of its quality process. Throughout the four-step process described shortly, Ford was constantly educating and training its work force in the ways of quality and, ultimately, customer satisfaction.

Petersen described a four-step program Ford introduced to create employee involvement and buy-in for their quality initiative. First, he opened up the books and encouraged managers and supervisors to start sharing information with all employees and other departments. Second, Ford organized steering committees at each facility comprised of five managers or supervisors and five hourly employees. These steering committees were charged with overseeing the employee involvement process and keeping an eye on its progress. Third, Petersen asked renowned quality guru, Dr. W. Edwards Deming, to consult with Ford and implement his famous Fourteen Points (see Table 6-1 for a listing of Dr. Deming's Fourteen Points). While Ford also relied on other outside consultants, it built on a core program which used the Deming principles as its foundation. Fourth and last, Ford looked for places to experiment. It wasn't concerned with being too scientific, according to Petersen, but rather used pilot projects where the quality process could be tested and refined. Then, it broadly introduced these processes throughout the company.

Table 6-1   The Deming Management Method: Fourteen Points*

1. Create constancy of purpose for the improvement of product and service.

2. Adopt the new philosophy (quality).

3. Cease dependence on mass inspection.

4. End the practice of awarding business on price tag alone.

5. Improve constantly and forever the system of production and service.

6. Institute training and retraining.

7. Institute leadership.

8. Drive out fear.

9. Break down barriers between staff areas.

10. Eliminate slogans, exhortations, and targets for the work force.

11. Eliminate numerical quotas.

12. Remove barriers to pride of workmanship.

13. Institute a vigorous program of education and retraining.

14. Take action to accomplish the transformation.

*Author's Note: For more insight on Dr. W. Edwards Deming and his management method, we refer you to Mary Walton's *The Deming Management Method* (New York: G.P. Putnam, 1986).

Employees and union leaders earned the respect of management, and in turn, the company generated greater worker productivity. This front-line commitment by Ford employees translated to building higher-quality cars. The public liked what it saw, and Ford has been able to capitalize on its commitment to quality. Ford has made its slogan "Quality Is Job One" a living practice.

The primary lesson to be learned—and there are many—is that the greatest incentive for the education and training of your employees is to ensure continued leadership excellence. It sounds like a cliche, but it continues to be true: "A company or organization is only as strong as its leaders."

▼ WANTED—LEADERS WITH A VISION

As a nation, we emulate our leaders. We look to our political, business, spiritual, social, and education leaders for meaning, purpose, and direction. But most important, we look to political and business leaders for *vision*—who we are, where we're going, and how we'll get there. Vision is the key.

The criteria that determine *how* successful a company will be ultimately can be measured by the leader's commitment to the education and training of his or her employees. A leader must educate and train himself or herself because a leader cannot teach others what he or she doesn't understand. In addition, the leader must strongly believe in the provision of an effective training process for employee growth and leadership development.

▼ THE EDUCATION OF A LEADER: FLEETWOOD ENTERPRISES' GLENN KUMMER

Although leaders are perceived as well-educated and progressive people, not all leaders are open to innovative ways of doing things and moving outside their comfort zone. But typically, when a company leader is progressive, constantly open to new ways, and always in search of meaningful ways to improve, the company—not surprisingly—prospers. One such leader is Glenn Kummer, President and COO of Fleetwood Enterprises. Kummer is not the *Fortune* 500 presidential stereotype. He believes strongly that there is good reason not to follow the status quo. It is because of Glenn Kummer's core belief that leaders must act and create momentum that Fleetwood Enterprises has become America's largest homebuilder.

Based in Riverside, California, Fleetwood, which ranks 270th on the *Fortune* 500 listing, specializes in constructing manufactured housing and building popular recreational vehicles.

Kummer, a 24-year veteran of Fleetwood, experienced the birth and development of the mobile housing and RV industries. As he grew through the ranks with Fleetwood, he had plenty of opportunities to test and validate Fleetwood founder John Crean's philosophy that "service, quality, and innovation were the hallmarks of a successful and profitable company." When the quality movement developed in corporate America, Kummer seized upon it and staked much of Fleetwood's future success on these basic principles.

In 1987, Kummer learned that some of his Housing Division product design engineers wanted to visit one of Fleetwood's suppliers which was making great strides in the areas of customer satisfaction and quality. That supplier was Milliken & Company located in Spartanburg, South Carolina. Two years later, Milliken & Company would gain recognition for its commitment to outstanding quality and customer satisfaction by winning the Malcolm Baldrige National Quality Award.

The report Glenn Kummer received from his product engineers on their site visit to Milliken prompted him to schedule a second visit for several key managers from Fleetwood's Housing Division and corporate management team. It was an eye-opening experience for all who attended. They saw firsthand how a company, dedicated to quality and service, could measure every aspect of its operations and reap high profits from customer satisfaction. It made a quality believer of Kummer and his senior managers.

Kummer, determined to build on this experience, encouraged all his corporate managers and Housing Division plant facility managers to attend Philip B. Crosby's Quality College in Winter Park, Florida. At the time, Crosby's consulting firm was sponsoring a week-long course on how to implement Crosby's own 14-point quality program.

After this indoctrination to customer-driven quality, Fleetwood's Housing Division management team created its own internal quality process and customer satisfaction measurement program. This step resulted in several major changes at Fleetwood.

First, every manager in the Housing Division was expected to adopt a quality improvement process based on the concepts learned at the Quality College course. Second, Fleetwood made a major commitment to implement a companywide customer satisfaction program which included hiring a former Crosby disciple, Jerry Hewitt, as vice president of quality. Not only was this a major commitment by Fleetwood, but it also sent a message. That message, as Jerry Hewitt told us, was that "because Fleetwood believes that quality impacts customer satisfaction, we are serious about measuring everything we do in terms of internal and external customer satisfaction. We also are committed for the long haul. This is not a program, but a lifelong process at Fleetwood."

John Pollis, Fleetwood's Director of Marketing, said, "The reason for our continuous quality improvement at Fleetwood is due to a sound philosophy from our chairman and the tenacity of our president to focus on it every day, every hour, at every meeting. At Fleetwood, quality isn't just an agenda item at management meetings. It's a core value that has become part of everything we plan and do."

Pollis also said that after five years, "the formal quality movement in our company is still evolving. But we are not discouraged because some companies including Milliken told us they've been working on their quality initiative for over ten years and, still, they are not where they want to be, ultimately! And, they're one of the best in America when it comes to understanding and applying a total quality process and satisfying their customers."

Kummer explained Fleetwood's challenge this way. "For Fleetwood," he said, "we faced several challenges early-on. One challenge was to create buy-in among our managers. This was true despite the fact that our housing division managers attended the Quality College.

Many of them also visited Milliken and experienced first-hand how quality could favorably impact customer satisfaction and bottom-line results. Nevertheless, it's one thing to see somebody else do it, yet another thing for you to actually do it."

To his credit, Glenn Kummer was very patient as a leader. But he constantly prodded and challenged Fleetwood's managers to stay focused on quality and customer satisfaction. This meant that Fleetwood had to earn the trust and respect of its own associates/employees.

"Internally, we believed the secret to earning the trust and support of our own associates was to make them an integral part of the quality process through measurements and a divisional awards program."

This strategy has paid off handsomely for Fleetwood Enterprises, which continues to enjoy higher than industry average sales and profits. We've really just begun to tap into our potential," said Jon Nord, Fleetwood's Senior Vice President of the Housing Division. He added, "We must constantly challenge our associates that they possess unlimited potential, despite limited company resources, to advance quality and customer satisfaction."

We share Jon Nord's belief. Unlike Fleetwood, too many companies think quality and service are money issues. While money and other resources are important to successfully launch a total quality process, the fact remains that people's commitment is the first, and most important, step. As Nord explained to us, "Had we listened to those little voices inside ourselves that said 'this is crazy, this isn't possible,' we would still be scratching our heads trying to figure out how we can improve our quality and raise our customer satisfaction levels. But, because we were challenged by Glenn and each other, and because we knew we could do a better job, we stepped out of our comfort zone and took some risks. Fortunately, it's paying off nicely for our company, our associates, our retailers, and our customers."

As Glenn Kummer told us, "every leader has the same responsibilities to his or her people. First, you need to be capable as a leader in order for people to follow you over the hill. This means a leader must always be open to learning new ways and how to improve himself or herself. Secondly, you need to have a plan—call it your vision or whatever term you want—but you need a clear direction and sense of purpose so people understand what you're trying to accomplish and what's expected of them. Finally, a leader has to be able to inspire and motivate people when things slow down or people get stuck. Creating momentum and helping people move past their self-imposed limitations, I think, is the key to achieving results. And, the most sought-after leaders are the ones who achieve their desired results."

▼ CHOOSING YOUR PATH TO TOTAL QUALITY

Training is the path every organization must travel if it wants to grow and prosper. A company must commit its time, money, and resources to teach its people the how's and why's of its mission, culture, and quality processes for getting the job done right the first time. And training must be an ongoing experiential process. Your training programs and curriculum must capture the newcomers and dip them in the corporate culture early on.

As one senior human resources director with a large financial services company told us, "When I came aboard, the number-crunchers and fixed budgets based on last year's expenses were driving this company. We had no clear plan. Employees were running off to seminars on everything from *Time Management* to *How to Manage Your Boss.* My in-box was flooded weekly with requests for these kinds of training sessions; and, not because we had major deficiencies in these areas, but because every department had a certain amount of money allocated to it for training and they were determined to spend it without too much regard for how it would improve their employee's customer satisfaction skills and the overall quality service at their office.

"Training budgets were driving our company's education process instead of our customers' needs. We changed all that by developing training criteria that were tied to our president's vision statement and the firm's mission statement. Without linking training into our vision and mission statement, it would not have been possible to get our department heads to focus on satisfying their customers' needs."

The way the company's human resources department got its training process back on track was to ask every department manager these two questions.

1. How will your department fulfill the company's vision and mission statements as they relate to your internal and external customers' needs?

2. By first surveying your employees, what are the specific professional development and skill building needs which are required of your employees in order to achieve our company's mission?

Training must be driven by the wants and needs of your customers. Your customer satisfaction program and quality process will identify the training your people require. Throughout many companies, we are witnessing a move away from generic training classes to a more carefully thought-out, unified curriculum which supports a company's quality process. This is the approach Federal Express, Uarco, Disney, and other companies have taken. And it works!

A retail executive expressed her feelings about corporate training this way. "We believe in training," she noted, "but not for the sake of training. If our employees can't identify their customers' needs, and articulate our company's strengths over the competition, and tell me in 25 words or less how we outperform our competition, all the training in the world won't help them increase their sales or delight their customers!"

Training should be driven by two factors. First, what do your people need to know that will help them be more successful in performing their jobs? Second, what areas have your customers identified that indicate your employees are lacking or need further skills to better serve them? It came as no surprise to us that these two factors are almost identical to the two questions asked by the bank's human resources director which we mentioned earlier.

The best way to answer these questions is to perform a training assessment. This is an activity your training staff should perform yearly. If you don't have a training department, an outside consultant can assist you in conducting a professional training assessment. The basic steps to follow are discussed next.

▼ TRAINING ASSESSMENT GUIDELINES

1. Tie your overall training program objectives to the corporate mission statement. Start by asking your department managers how their present training programs complement the company's mission statement or CEO's vision.

2. Review and understand the processes and interfaces of all employee job functions; assess the skill level and training each employee currently receives. This requires all supervisors and managers to know their associates, and it mandates that every manager develop a professional growth track for his or her associates. It also requires—at the minimum—quarterly goal setting and feedback sessions to measure progress and goal attainment.

3. Conduct an employee assessment to determine the training needs of your employees and whether their needs are being met. The challenge here for most managers and supervisors is "Where do I begin?" One assessment form we like comes from Gerry Brummit, President of Cybernetics Leadership Center in Coronado. Gerry developed his Internal Organizational Survey as a means of helping management determine exactly what employees liked or disliked about their company. By identifying 30 categories, which employees rank on a scale which ranges from outstanding to very poor, Gerry can show where rifts or differences exist between customers, employees, and management. Here is a listing of the 30 categories he asks nonmanagers and managers to rank:

1. Individual motivation/initiative/pride in work
2. Technical skills and competence

3. Management and leadership skills
4. Individual commitment to quality in work
5. Understanding the mission and purpose of the company
6. Time use/productivity
7. Effectiveness of meetings
8. Teamwork/cooperation/trust
9. Openness to ideas/feedback/change
10. Delegation from top down to lower ranks
11. Communication (down, up, and across)
12. Data gathering to support planning
13. Setting goals and planning for results
14. Departmental goal achievement
15. Problem solving/autonomous decision making
16. Meeting deadlines
17. Organizational structure/role/clarity
18. Policies, rules, and procedures
19. Systems for analyzing work flow
20. Mutual support between departments/sections
21. Overall quality, productivity, and performance
22. Cost consciousness/budget management
23. Attention to needs/aspirations of people
24. Encouragement of professional growth
25. Personal and leadership development emphasis
26. Recognition and rewards for performance
27. Openness/warmth/support
28. Overall attitude and morale
29. Company's commitment to continuous improvement/quality
30. Orientation and responsiveness to customers

Gerry also asks every employee to list three things they like about their company and three things the employee would like to see changed or improved. Armed with this information, a manager or executive can not only quickly identify the training gaps, but also target specific areas that might be trouble spots between rank and file employees and management.

4. Conduct a customer assessment to determine if your customers feel your employees possess the necessary technical skills and human relations training and product knowledge to provide them with excellent service. We've addressed several ways this can be accomplished. The only other comment we would add to reinforce this important step is "just do it."

5. Recommend, plan, and implement a comprehensive training program based on the requirements identified in steps 1–4. The importance of this step is that it forces you to think through your training process before you can begin to train your people.

▼ FIVE STEPS FOR CREATING AN EFFECTIVE EDUCATION AND TRAINING PROGRAM

There are five steps in creating an effective education and training program for your employees, suppliers, and customers:

1. Determine what type of training to provide your people.
2. Devise a progressive education and training curriculum that yields long-term results for your people.
3. Deliver education and training to your employees.
4. Train your customers and suppliers in the ways of doing business with your company.
5. Measure the effectiveness of your training and make any necessary changes where it is not effective.

1. Determine What Type of Training to Provide Your People

First, ask your customers about the service performance of your employees. Frequently invite them to give their opinions and comments through a combination of evaluation sessions, focus groups, comment cards, telephone surveys, and direct response surveys. Perform these assessments on a regular basis. Encourage your customers to tell you what you're doing right and what you're doing wrong. Remember that your customer feedback sessions or assessment processes need not be complicated. More important is getting the information you need to establish training priorities.

Once you have this information act quickly to conduct training and education programs that will bring about the necessary changes to improve your employees' service performance and their attitudes and behavior.

Second, allow your non-management employees/associates to evaluate and critique the company's overall performance and determine where training will improve their productivity, skill levels, and/or customer awareness. By encouraging front-line employees to help determine training needs, you will allow them to shape their own destiny. A healthy organization invites introspection. It wants to help its people grow and develop. To retain your "best and brightest" employees, it is imperative to offer an ongoing series of personal development and professional growth programs that will challenge them to think smarter and outperform the competition.

Finally, invite your suppliers to be part of the education and training process. As the producers and suppliers of your goods and services, suppliers should be treated as partners in your success. We have witnessed an outgrowth of positive involvement between companies and their vendors since the inception of the Malcolm Baldrige National Quality Award. Companies such as Milliken, Motorola, and Xerox are requiring their suppliers to test their quality and service standards against the Baldrige Award criteria to retain their supplier status. We view this as a healthy process because, ultimately, a company is only as good as its suppliers and vendors. Substandard suppliers can cause a company to fail and ultimately lose its customers.

2. Devise a Progressive Education and Training Curriculum That Yields Long-Term Results for Your People

Build upon the results of your internal and external assessments. Next, consider the business you're in. What levels of training do your people need to succeed? For most organizations, training can be divided into three categories: human relations skills, technical competency, and quality measurement processes.

Human Relations Skills

This level of training reflects the people-to-people skills such as courtesy, empathy, listening and communication, and general human relations skills.

Technical Competency

Technically, your people must have all the tools, equipment, and training necessary to perform their jobs. At Isuzu Truck of America, we've seen how their corporate managers and district representatives have worked closely with their dealers to ensure that every dealership has trained technicians who understand the complexity of product changes and, most important, whom to contact in order to get answers to their technical questions. We've also seen how Isuzu Truck of America simplified terms and technical jargon for its customers so that the typical truck owner or driver would understand the repair work performed and the services provided by the technicians.

On the consumer product side, we think the General Electric Answer Center, a consumer hotline service that is staffed 24 hours a day, 365 days a year, epitomizes the kind of commitment companies should be making to their valued customers. For example, at the Louisville GE center, carefully selected employees receive over a month's training prior to being placed in a customer-contact role. Employees also enjoy ongoing training to enhance their skills and product knowledge. When employees understand the technical aspects of a product, customer loyalty and sales will increase. One important note here. Our definition of technical training extends to all disciplines within a company, including sales, marketing, finance, human resources, and administrative functions. It also includes both exempt and nonexempt personnel.

Quality Measurement Processes

The area of quality measurement processes has taken on greater significance in the training arena thanks to the growing awareness and importance of total quality as it affects customer satisfaction. The most important reason for training your people in quality measurement processes is to help them improve the quality of the products and services they create so that their customers' expectations are met or exceeded.

Once your people understand quality measurement processes, they will be more likely to recommend changes that improve the quality of your products. This will help your people better understand the relationship between what they produce and how customer satisfaction is created. We encourage companies to amend their training curriculums to address this important area.

3. Deliver Education and Training to Your Employees

Training need not be limited to a classroom setting. In fact, we are seeing more and more training conducted on sales calls, on the shop floor, and along the manufacturing assembly line. Many companies are changing their training focus from the theoretical teaching methods to "how-to" classes based on customer feedback and employee assessments.

There is a true sense of urgency among companies to get results. Training managers are seeking new ways to impact the bottom line to minimize the amount of time away from the job. The reason for this change should be obvious. You cannot serve your customers if you're not there! On the other hand, you cannot adequately serve your customers unless you are superbly trained.

We encourage your company to raise the bar of excellence by applying innovative training techniques internally. We also encourage you to implement a mentoring program so that the wisdom and experience of long-term employees isn't lost. Part of what we want our people to learn is how the company grew and prospered over the years. This is something that only your veterans can teach. Give them that opportunity. You will find it reenergizes them as well.

At ITT-Bowest, AT&T Universal Card Services, and other progressive companies, employee orientations and video messages from their CEO are used to help teach newcomers the values and culture cherished by the organization. This type of training, while more attitudinal, is just as important to an employee's long-term success and job satisfaction.

4. Train Your Customers and Suppliers in the Ways of Doing Business with Your Company

(Also, train your front-line people in communicating this to your customers and suppliers.)

Your company must play a proactive role in consumer education. Product instructions should be easy to read. Catalogs must provide useful, customer information. Salespersons need to be better trained and understand what they're selling.

Today, more factory representatives are available to provide 30-minute instructional classes to retail employees before their stores open. Toll-free answer centers are plugging in across the country to help consumers understand the many benefits and uses of a particular product.

At Fleetwood Enterprises, we witnessed the entire Housing Division sales force undergo a lengthy training and orientation from their carpet supplier, Carriage Carpets. Several new carpet materials were being introduced and Fleetwood arranged for Carriage Carpets' sales representatives to explain the benefits and features of the new line.

At Nordstrom, we've regularly seen suppliers gather the retailer's sales associates in a circle and spend 30 minutes prior to opening explaining the sales features of a product line.

While visiting Fleetwood's Dream Center, we saw how housing representatives put their training and feedback to the company's advantage. Because the Dream Center is located across the freeway from a competitor's factory and headquarters, it attracts a large number of prospective homeowners who visit both sites. One day, a visitor to the Fleetwood Dream Center remarked that "too many manufactured homes were poorly constructed." After Fleetwood's housing representative explained to the visitor the facts about the outstanding quality construction and materials used to build Fleetwood homes, the visitor said, "How would I know . . . I can't see the stuff you're talking about." Taking a cue from this visitor, Fleetwood sent in a crew to cut away a section of the flooring, walls, and ceiling to display the high quality of the construction and materials. Now, when a prospective homebuyer or curious visitor tours the Dream Center, he or she can see how the home is constructed. It reminds us of the saying, "I can't define quality, but I know it when I see it!"

Quality can no longer be left to chance. Every company that wishes to make a serious commitment to total quality and customer satisfaction must institute the broadest possible training program for its employees, customers, and suppliers.

5. Measure the Effectiveness of Your Training

Many companies offer their employees training programs. But, is this training effective? Does it make any difference in how well an employee performs his or her job? How do you know whether or not your training is effective?

To measure the effectiveness of your training, begin by identifying those who are affected by the training. This could be external customers, internal customers, managers of students, suppliers, and so on.

If you survey your employees, ask them if the training they've received has made any measurable difference in how well they perform their duties or in the quality of the work they deliver to their internal customers. Ask your internal customers if they've noticed a measurable change in the quality of your work. Subsequent to any large-scale training program, find out from your *external* customers if the training has had a positive impact in how you conduct business with them.

Companies that have progressed beyond this point have sophisticated measurement devices they are using to determine the effectiveness of their training and make improvements based on their findings. We encourage you to seek out these companies through your local chapter of the American Society for Training & Development (ASTD) located in Alexandria, Virginia, or the American Society for Quality Control in Milwaukee, Wisconsin.

▼ THE HARRIS BANK TRAINING PROGRAM: POSITIONING AGAINST THE COMPETITION

Once a company embarks on its quest for quality, how does it stay the course? One way is to use ongoing professional development and training programs that further the company's vision and commitment to quality. This is how Harris Bank, headquartered in Chicago, is positioning itself against its competition.

Harris Bank has cultivated a strong internal commitment to quality. As we implied earlier, a *progressive* company is a company or organization that has made an irrevocable commitment to becoming best-in-class and is dedicating its resources and people to achieve a customer-focused reputation. This definition fits Harris Bank. Like most companies, Harris Bank did not know what hurdles and difficulties they would have to overcome on the road to becoming customer focused and quality driven. But, instinctively, their leaders knew it was both the right course and, perhaps, the only course that would ensure their future security and success. Figure 6-1 illustrates Harris Bank's guiding principles.

Figure 6-1 Harris Bank
Source: Harris Bank, © Harris Trust and Savings Bank. Chicago, Illinois.

Six Guiding Principles for Creating Leadership Buy-in and Commitment

Harris Bank Chairman B. Kenneth West set the tone and vision for his managers in 1991 when he told them:

> Our anchor to stability in the midst of change will be a set of six guiding principles which we, as a Leadership Team, have developed together. We believe that if we do these six things exceedingly well, we will hold the keys to our long-term competitive success.

1. The customer's voice drives all actions of the organization.
2. Produce consistently positive results through well-designed and well-managed processes.
3. Develop and empower people to exceed customers' expectations.
4. Deliver value to our customers through teamwork.
5. Recognize that everything can and must be continuously improved.
6. Make the improvement of quality and the elimination of waste the daily goal of the organization.

Taking On the Challenge of Becoming Customer Focused

One thing the Harris organization learned along the way from other companies that were implementing a customer-focused process was that developing a common language and a common understanding of total customer focus was paramount to its success. As a result, the Training Team was the first team launched.

Karen Stoeller, a Harris vice president, recalls the day she was asked to take on the challenge. "I was called to a meeting one day along with some of my colleagues, and Harris's senior leadership said, 'We want you to head the training team, and we want you to coordinate the training for total customer focus.' That was it. I thought for a moment and said to them, 'I'm not sure what that means,' and they responded,

'We're not sure what it means, either. But we know what we want to accomplish based on 18 months of site visits and researching what can be achieved if we commit to a total customer focus process.' "

Karen continued, "I asked our senior leadership if they would be willing to give us some guidelines that define what we want Harris Bank employees to do relative to this process. This would give our training team a starting point. They agreed, and we ended up with a two and one-half page white paper that basically told us what types of behaviors senior management wanted to see in the daily behavior of Harris Bank employees. It also included what behaviors top leaders expected from managers.

"We took that document and spent approximately five days with our Senior Management Team just questioning and probing on all the points. We spent hours on hours asking them to expound on what they meant by this statement or that phrase. We just went through that iteration process of trying to clarify more specifically what they had written on that two and one-half page white paper."

Anyone who has sat through intense meetings knows that listening is an exhaustive exercise. Karen described the energy drain this way. "There were days [during this initial process] when we would say to the Steering Committee at about 2:00 P.M., 'We know we'll have more questions, but we're tired, we need to go think about all this . . . .' But they hung in there with us and that's what ultimately made the process work for us. When you can corral the chairman, the president, and the three top officers of the bank and spend this amount of time, eventually you'll get it right!"

So, what direction should you take in your questions and exploratory discussions with your company's leadership? Stephen King of Harris Bank had this response based on his own experience. "We had a very specific goal in mind. We knew that if our training was going to be successful it could not be driven by broad issues. It must be behavioral. By this I mean we wanted to understand the behaviors our leadership was hoping to engender into the organization through training. We asked them to describe a manager or supervisor who was acting in a way that was empowering others. This was an easy one. Defining how someone managed a process was much tougher."

Harris's leadership team adopted 17 behavioral statements that clearly defined what was expected of every employee in the organization. This has become the foundation from which most of their training is derived.

Launching the Six Core Harris Training Program

In its first year, the Harris program included six core training programs:

1. *Customer Value Analysis:* Learning how to listen effectively to customers and clarify their expectations.

2. *Measurement:* Learning to measure process.

3. *Gap Analysis:* Learning to determine the cause of the gap between customers' expectations and their assessment of the actual service.

4. *Decision Making:* Learning to select the best means of closing the service gap.

5. *Planning and Implementing:* Learning to implement decisions.

6. *Continuous Improvement:* Learning to improve processes continuously through the application of the training process behaviors.

When it came time to offer the training, it was thought that the managers should be trained first. The general feeling was that if the managers understood it, they could reinforce it throughout the workplace with their people. As Karen Stoeller explained it, "Our managers wanted to be first in everything we did. So the original idea was to train them as a group and then the training would cascade down through the different levels of management and, eventually, the rest of the organization." But that scenario never happened.

Treat Management and Nonmanagement the Same

Karen explained how the front-line employees taught management a valuable lesson. "When we created our first pilot program, we decided to assemble a cross section of 100 employees from throughout the bank. At these sessions, we described what the senior managers wanted to do. The reaction was very strong against the notion of treating non-managers as a separate class. We could see that a number of employees were reacting 'Here we go again. They're treating us as a separate class in this organization and so on.' So, we went back to our internal customer (the Leadership Team) and we gave them this feedback. To their credit, they understood the situation quickly and suggested we conduct the training differently. Now, we have managers scattered throughout the courses including our chairman. He just shows up like every other employee and this has had a very positive, powerful impact on the program."

Six of the eight training curriculums are for all employees. Two additional courses were designed specifically for managers. It took one group ten months to complete its eight classes. Each class is one day followed by a three-week guided practice period during which the group receives an assignment to work on with a coach. The members return to the classroom for a half-day follow-up session. The two "management-only" classes are full-day sessions.

Stephen King emphasized the importance of the first course in the total customer focus (TCF) curriculum entitled customer value analysis (CVA). He told us, "If there is a course in this curriculum that is a customer service course, this is it. CVA is all about customer expectations. The course pivots around who is your customer? What does he or she expect from you? What are you actually delivering to your customers? Is there a service gap and, if so, how can you characterize it? So, what we do is spend a great deal of time talking about the notion of who is the customer and the give and take in the relationship. Some employees find the whole notion of having a customer rather strange. But we discuss this at length because we cannot move forward until this issue is clearly resolved—and favorably so—in our minds."

Figure 6-2 on page 168 depicts how customers figure in the circular value chain at Harris Bank.

Each course program has a detailed workbook that reinforces the training material presented in the classroom. Stephen King described the importance of the training materials to the successful introduction

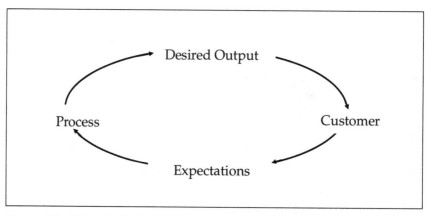

Figure 6-2 Value Chain-Harris Bank

of the TCF process. "We were much more interested in picturing circles in people's minds," King told us. He added, "This is why we selected the circular graphic. This graphic demonstrates the importance of the customer in everything we do at The Harris. Customers establish their requirements as well as their expectations of the process, our products, and the employee interplay with them. The beauty of this graphic is that it fits every training course and serves as the basis for every conversation we have. There's no escaping the question of who are your customers and what do they expect from you."

The Harris Bank management training programs deal with managing and coaching TCF behaviors. Again, in the first management course, Harris trainers drive home the overriding questions:

- Who are your customers?
- What do they expect from you?
- What are you actually delivering?
- Is there a customer service gap here?

These types of questions force managers to confront early on the perceptions of their employees. This exercise, it is hoped, results in people understanding the duality of a relationship. For so many years, businesses have viewed customer relations as a process during which an employee gives something to another person, namely, a customer. But, in reality, there is a dual expectation. Not only should the customer have an expectation, but so should the employee and manager. That employee expectation can range from a friendly encounter to satisfaction or, ultimately, "wowing" a customer by exceeding his or her expectations.

▼ CALCULATING THE COST OF CREATING A CUSTOMER-FOCUSED PROCESS

One question that frequently is asked of companies like Harris Bank is, "What will it cost us to make the transition from our present operating method to a more customer-focused, quality-driven approach?" Perhaps the answer can be found by twisting the question to, "What will it cost us *not* to become a totally customer-focused company?" One thing that strikes us about companies like Harris Bank and other quality-committed companies is that they realize that there is a greater cost *not* to make the transition from operations-driven and bureaucratic stagnation to a customer-focused, quality-driven way of doing business. The competition isn't going to stand still nor will your customers remain loyal to your business if someone is building a better mousetrap and providing a more pleasant service experience to boot!

Karen Stoeller said this about computing the cost of training: "I don't need to worry ever about computing the costs of training or what a TCF process is going to cost because my customers are doing that for me! The minute I say we're going to have a nine-day training program, I can tell you that every manager in this bank has figured out how many lost days of productivity that really represents. But the beauty of our assignment was that we were shielded from this and other valid arguments because management said everybody is going through this program—like it or not. So, frankly, it didn't matter. Yes, we crammed it into a short time span but, that too, yielded benefits. It created momentum in our organization. And that's critical to achieving success!"

The truth to tabulating the real cost of becoming a totally customer- focused company is nearly impossible. How does a company begin to calculate the hours of preparation necessary to design a TCF-related process? While the number of classroom hours required of your employees can be measured, how does a company begin to measure unknown variables such as lost customers and lost business opportunities resulting from your inability to provide them with a positive service experience?

We've concluded that a company cannot successfully implement a total quality service process if it is concerned about operating within a very restricted dollar budget. That being said, we also realize resources are limited. The implementation of quality must be sold on the basis that, over the long term, quality is free. Quality must be considered an investment in the same way equipment, buildings, refurbishments, and so forth are considered requirements of doing business. Like these examples, quality improvements can be delayed, but the longer they are delayed, the more expensive they will become, and the longer it will take to achieve the payback which will come from increased productivity. And that payback is often more directly countable than equipment, buildings, and refurbishments. The dollars are not only real additions to the bottom line; they are cumulative.

▼ QUALITY TAKES TIME

Another lesson we've learned from quality leaders in other companies is that *true quality* takes time. When we asked Karen what it costs in terms of time, money, and human resources to establish a total quality service program, she said, "If people knew, they wouldn't do it!"

But what it costs not to do it could mean significant loss in market share. Plus, over the long-term the countable benefits almost always exceed expectations.

▼ LESSONS LEARNED

One lesson from the Harris Bank story is: "You must strike while the iron is hot." Senior managers don't want yet another program or directive; their calendars are already overloaded. It's a matter of moving things around so that the issue of total quality service takes precedence over other matters. The role of the champion is to convince corporate executives that a commitment to total customer focus will deliver a greater return on investment than other programs and expenditures.

Another lesson learned from the Harris Bank story is that Harris went outside its banking industry to establish its goal for total customer focus. Karen admits that Harris did little or no benchmarking in the banking industry. In fact it tied the training process to customer expectations rather than what other companies (and banks) were already doing. This approach paid off in two ways. First, it developed a state-of-the-art training program, probably better than one they could have gotten elsewhere. Second, later on, when the usual skepticism surfaced in the classroom during the first weeks of training, there was incredible buy-in from the trainers.

The trainers caught the backlash of comments and negative messages that were directed at the senior managers who had tried the customer-focused approach before but without success. Rather than toe the party line, the trainers stood up and said, "We don't know if our chairman is going to make this process live at Harris Bank. But we do know we believe in it and use it and practice it." Then the trainers shared their experiences with this process and related their successes and failures so that the other employees saw it through the eyes of people who truly believed in the program.

Another lesson learned from the Harris Bank story is perseverance. Karen Stoeller told us of the one class she taught where people were complaining. She said to them, " 'If our chairman comes to me and says, Karen, I want you to do the cause analysis on why this program isn't working, the first place I'm going to look is right here with the managers in this organization. It's my responsibility as a fellow manager to set the pace, tone, and consistency around this organization. So if it isn't working this will be the first place I come looking to ask you people what you've done to make it successful. It is your job.' I just felt somebody had to stand up and make that pronouncement."

▼ REALIZING THE "AHA'S" OF QUALITY-DRIVEN SERVICE

Some of the important gains companies have realized by implementing a quality service process included the obvious. For example, one manager told us about two employees who were conducting an internal customer interview as part of their assessment process.

After five minutes these two employees realized they were duplicating functions, doing the same thing although for different purposes. Now they are able to combine their functions, which saves time, money, and increases their productivity. When your people go out and ask their internal and external customers to define *their* expectations as opposed to asking a customer only what he or she thinks about you, or about the things you consider important, the interview takes on a new slant, providing a more valuable exchange of ideas and insights.

Another "Aha" to be learned from Harris Bank's approach to total customer focus is the importance of *teaching behavior* to your employees. What Harris Bank developed is a course based on real-life, day-to-day issues their employees handle. Stephen King told us how he goes from one department to the next searching for meaningful examples of things going on in the bank. This way, Harris Bank's training is both relevant and customized to suit the needs of the employees sitting in the classrooms.

Homework is an important part of learning and retention of training information. Every Harris Bank employee who attends the various one-day courses completes a homework assignment. Every employee is assigned a coach and is asked to work with his or her coach to complete the homework assignment. Once this is done, employees attend a final half-day training program to complete their course training loop. The best homework assignments are incorporated into a future training course. This way, Harris Bank is constantly updating its training material with fresh ideas and new case studies that appeal to a broad spectrum of employees.

Another thing Harris Bank learned is that not every employee can relate to cash management. However, everyone is expected to understand how a checking account is opened and managed as well as how to perform important support staff functions such as ordering items out of a stockroom to keep the front-line employees well equipped and stocked.

The Harris Organization epitomizes what every business can achieve once it commits to the process of creating a total quality service process. Like other companies, Harris Bank struggled as it found its way through the customer-focus maze. But, unlike some companies, Harris Bank never gave up. Today, it is championing the quality service process because several quality champions had the courage to tough it out and stick with this process.

Karen Stoeller said it better than anyone when she told us, "If the successful companies really knew what it would take to turn their organizations around before they committed to this process, most of them never would have begun the quality service journey because they would have doubted their own ability to accomplish it." While we share that view, we also know that the cost of *not* addressing your customers' needs through a quality service process can be a mistake, which could be fatal to your business.

In summary

- Effective education and training requires strong leadership—leadership which recognizes the importance of education to ensure a company's future strength.

- Your training and education should be related to the wants and needs of your customers and your employees' requirements for serving customers.

- Institute a training assessment that is tied to your overall objectives and ensures that your curriculum yields positive results.

- Learn to improve continuously through the application of training to your processes.

CHAPTER SEVEN

Leading by Example: How to Achieve a Corporate Reputation for Quality

Nothing attracts and keeps customers like a genuine commitment to quality and service excellence.

Many companies, nonprofit organizations, and government agencies have come to our attention because they gained a reputation for *doing things right*. These companies have pockets of excellence which their customers recognize and brag about to other prospective customers.

We selected these organizations because we found at least one common thread throughout the entire group. All these entities have people who are going *above and beyond the call of duty* to ensure that a quality process takes root internally. In our eyes these people are champions. In nearly every instance they've succeeded, or they are well on their way to success. We should add that none of these champions has escaped their share of failures along the way.

Most champions launch their quest for quality with a singular purpose in mind—to achieve excellence in their department or division. Eventually, as the results become obvious, the movement blossoms into a companywide commitment. We've cited some of the service and quality champions who have overcome great odds to help establish their company as a best-in-class organization. The pockets of excellence we will share with you give credence to the argument that quality and customer satisfaction are first and foremost a *people-driven* effort. We find the initial emphasis must be on people, pride, and performance rather than on profits, productivity, and percentages.

The end result for these organizations has been a higher level of customer satisfaction and improved quality. Their degree of success varies. But defining their success isn't our primary purpose at this time. Rather, we hope you'll take note of the kinds of things people are doing to improve quality and service in their organizations and make a difference in the lives of their employees and customers.

▼ UARCO INC. (BARRINGTON, ILLINOIS)

A Total Quality Strategy

Uarco is a company whose primary business is customized business forms, both paper and automated. The company is headquartered in Barrington, Illinois.

The business forms industry is intensely competitive. But Uarco has always been a tough competitor. Realizing that the marketplace would get tougher instead of easier because of shifting customers' needs and the advent of computer technology, Uarco made a commitment to excellence by adopting a total quality program in 1990. Larry Dille, a seasoned veteran of the company since 1959, was named Vice President, Education/Standards of Excellence. It was Larry's responsibility to direct Uarco's Commitment to Excellence program.

The significance of appointing a seasoned "company man" to the task turned out to be a smart move for two reasons. First, Larry knew and understood the inner workings of Uarco. As an officer of the company he had clout and could make things happen. Additionally, he already oversaw the education and training program of the company.

In Larry's favor was Uarco's philosophy and cultural commitment to quality. Uarco customized its manufacturing process based on the philosophies of Deming and Juran combined with the Baldrige

Award criteria which emphasize the importance of leadership and customer satisfaction. Uarco's executives also went back to the classroom to learn the total quality practices from Baldrige winners including Motorola and Xerox.

▼ UARCO'S VISION AND MISSION STATEMENT

Uarco's vision, which supports the company's commitment to total quality is: "Our vision is to be the best in all we do as judged by our customers, employees, and suppliers, and to be the envy of our competitors."

Uarco's mission reads: "Our mission is to design, manufacture, warehouse, and distribute a full line of value-added business forms and provide related products and services to businesses, institutions, and selected government entities in North America.

Uarco stated its expected results:

1. Satisfied and loyal customers

2. Increased market share

3. High growth

4. Superior financial strength

5. Increased opportunities for our customers, employees, and suppliers

Larry Dille chaired a steering committee of 11 key executives. Four areas were identified to help Uarco achieve excellence:

1. Customer focus

2. Cycle time reduction

3. Error-free work

4. Partnerships with customers, employees, and suppliers

Larry and his steering committee began by trying to identify what needed to be accomplished. Then they examined the best way to attain their total quality goal. Finally, they developed a plan, sought commitment and buy-in from colleagues, and began implementing the total quality strategy throughout Uarco.

Uarco's Biggest Challenge: Employee Involvement

Larry defined Uarco's biggest challenge as employee involvement. As he told us, "Each employee is asking, 'How does commitment to excellence affect me?' My biggest challenge is having everyone recognize how his or her performance affects the program and, ultimately, customer satisfaction."

Another challenge Larry faced was the argument from all levels that Uarco was already committed to quality. He responded, "Our company has always been committed to quality. In fact, we've always prided ourselves on producing quality work. But, the reality of today's competitive marketplace is that Uarco—and every other company for that matter—must improve on what it's already doing in order to remain competitive and pull ahead of the competition. For us it comes down to a new, finer focus on quality."

When we asked Larry about creating a commitment to excellence, he said, "A commitment to excellence is bigger than product quality. Its long-term thrust is satisfying customers' needs. As I see it, Uarco has two types of customers—external and internal. The external customer is the person who buys your products. The internal customer is the person who receives your work. For example, if you're a press person, the finishing operator is your internal customer. Understanding the needs of the person who receives your work is important in establishing a total quality system."

Uarco clearly understands that its quality system stretches beyond simply manufacturing a product. It has expanded its definition of quality to include "from the time the salesperson anticipates a customer's needs to the time the customer *happily* pays the invoice." And, now, everybody at Uarco understands the critical role he or she plays in achieving that enviable end result—a happy customer. As Larry told us, "Quality has moved beyond the print floor into the corporate office. *We no longer think of quality strictly in terms of order entry to shipping the product. It's everybody's job."*

Another thing we noticed in our conversations with Larry was his genuine excitement about Uarco's total quality process. It was refreshing to see him get excited about the risks that his company was undertaking. And Larry's enthusiasm has been contagious. His staff and others throughout Uarco not only subscribe to the total quality process, but they are benefiting from it by putting it to their everyday use.

Uarco also adopted a means of measuring its results, they dubbed it the "2 × 2 System"—*double the quality by reducing the number of defects in half.*

Problem-Solving Techniques at Uarco

We share with you just one way Uarco has improved its overall quality as a result of this long-term plan. The example, Problem-Solving Techniques, comes from Steve Diller, Uarco's Coordinator of Education and Total Quality. Steve has earned the nickname "quality pest" thanks to his relentless pursuit of making the Commitment to Excellence program stick.

Uarco believes that the basis of every total quality program is a problem-solving method. The problem-solving method should contain specific steps to be used to reduce or eliminate any defect which causes customer dissatisfaction. Here is how Uarco approaches problem solving.

The Real-Win-Worth Approach

Uarco pays tribute to other quality companies that have paved the way with their problem-solving techniques. Uarco tailored these techniques to develop the first part of its problem-solving method. The company refers to it as the real-win-worth approach. It involves asking three key questions and each has a subset of questions. They are:

1. Is it real?
   - What do we want to change?
   - What are we doing now?

2. Can we win?
   - How can we make the change?
   - Who will do what?
   - When can we do it?

3. Is it worth it?
   - How do we know the solution is effective?
   - How well did it work?

▼ THE V-I-S-I-O-N PROBLEM-SOLVING METHOD

The real-win-worth formula has become the driving force of Uarco's "V-I-S-I-O-N" problem-solving method. "VISION" is an acronym that has corresponding questions for each step of the problem-solving method (See Figure 7-1 on page 183):

Visualize the problem.
Q. What do we want to change?

Identify a baseline.
Q. What are we doing now?

Strategize and plan a solution.
Q. How can we make the change?

Implement your solution.
Q. Who will do what? When can we do it?

Organize evaluation methods.
Q. How do we know if it's effective?

Note your results.
Q. How well did it work?

The "Luck of the Irish" Application to Problem Solving

One example that Uarco uses to illustrate how well the VISION problem-solving method works hails from a legendary Notre Dame football game. Not only does this example demonstrate how the problem-solv-

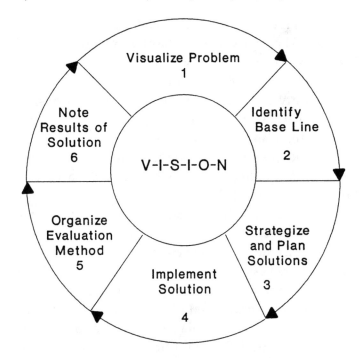

Is It Real?
1. What do we want to change?
2. What are we doing now?

Can We Win?
3. How can we make the change?
4. Who will do what? When can we do it?

Is It Worth It?
5. How do we know the solution is effective?
6. How well did it work?

Figure 7-1   V-I-S-I-O-N Problem-Solving Model
Source: Uarco Inc.

ing method can be used internally, but also, as Uarco demonstrated, it can be a "fun" exercise to get your people thinking in terms of solving their own quality-related problems.

If you are a long-time college football fan, perhaps you recall the game. The year was 1975. Notre Dame was playing Air Force. The Irish were expected to win hands down, but by the end of the third quarter, Notre Dame's quarterback, Rick Slager, had passed the ball only 32 yards, thrown two interceptions, and lost two fumbles. Air Force had massed a 20-point advantage and led the game 30-10. In short, Notre Dame's passing attack was ineffective and mistake prone. This made their attempts to run the ball also ineffective. Should Notre Dame stick with a running attack or throw more passes? Perhaps they should change quarterbacks? These were the questions Notre Dame's coaching staff were asking themselves.

Notre Dame decided to change to a "passing attack" strategy. This was their best chance to overcome the lopsided 19-point differential. However, their starting quarterback had been ineffective. So they brought in an untested player named Joe Montana who had a better throwing arm than Slager, according to the team's offensive coordinator. Notre Dame's offense picked up momentum and seemed to rally around Montana, who responded by racking up 146 passing yards and scoring 21 unanswered points in 7 minutes and 3 seconds. There were no more Notre Dame turnovers and by the end of the game, Notre Dame had rallied behind Joe Montana to pull out a 31-30 victory!

Let's assume you're the coach at Notre Dame. It's late in the third quarter. You're faced with the same problem and so you resort to Uarco's V-I-S-I-O-N problem-solving method to turn a losing situation into a potential winner. Here's how you might apply Uarco's V-I-S-I-O-N problem-solving method under these circumstances:

1. *Visualize your problem.* What do we want to change? Our passing game is ineffective. We're running out of time, and we need to control the ball and score fast.

2. *Identify Base Line.* What are we doing now? Rick Slager has passed for 32 yards, thrown two interceptions, and fumbled twice in the game.

3. *Strategize and plan.* How can we make the change? After brainstorming, we have three options: (1) continue our running game, (2) switch to a passing game with Slager, or (3) replace Slager with Joe Montana, who the offensive coordinator rates better as a passing quarterback. The Montana solution (3) was chosen.

4. *Implement solution.* Who will do what? Montana will replace Slager as quarterback. When can we do it? The switch will be made immediately—with little time remaining in the third quarter.

5. *Organize evaluation methods.* How do we know our solution will be effective? The scoreboard, quarterback statistics (and the cheering or booing of the fans) will measure Montana's performance.

6. *Note results.* How well did it work? The final game score was 31-30 in Notre Dame's favor. Montana passed for 146 yards, with no interceptions and no fumbles to score 21 points in 7 minutes and 3 seconds.

As you can see from Uarco's V-I-S-I-O-N problem-solving method, the critical part is "strategizing and planning solutions." This step involves brainstorming. Notre Dame's head coach, out of desperation, probably consulted his coaching staff to brainstorm for options before deciding to send in the rookie quarterback, Joe Montana.

Five Guidelines When Brainstorming for Answers

Although most situations in corporate life differ from the one facing Notre Dame's football team, the V-I-S-I-O-N approach is adaptable to many varied situations. It can be used to find new ways to increase sales, change a manufacturing or engineering process, or create innovative products.

Whenever you begin to brainstorm, we recommend you follow these guidelines to help you toward a successful outcome:

1. *Specifically identify the problem.* This will keep your attention on the issues at hand and help you avoid wasting time debating inconsequential issues.

2. *Choose a moderator and a recorder.* A conscientious scribe is needed along with the moderator whose role is to keep the group focused on the central problem.

3. *Involve all group members.* The moderator's second role is to ensure every attendee has a chance to participate. The more ideas, the better the discussion and, ultimately, the solution. Make sure everyone present is involved in the conversation.

4. *Avoid evaluation and negating off-the-wall ideas.* That comes later. But at this stage you want to stimulate the creative process, not kill it. So don't!

5. *Strive for quantity (not the quality) of ideas.* "Piggyback" ideas. Remember, no idea is a bad idea at this point. Even the most ridiculous suggestions can spark someone's imagination and offer the best solution. So tolerate any and all ideas.

How the PPC Method Can Help You Find the Best Solution

Uarco's quality team developed a unique method which we think is worth sharing. It's called the PPC Method. Here's the key. Evaluate the *plus* or advantages of the solution. Determine its *potential* in future gains or spin-offs and discuss any *concerns* or drawbacks your group may have about the solution. Remember, always express concerns in the form of a question. For example, you might ask, "How will we objectively measure the solutions?" instead of stating emphatically, "That idea won't work . . . there's no way to measure the results!" By stating your concern in the form of a question, the originator of the idea won't be insulted or put off by your comment.

What if . . . Brainstorming for the Perfect Bathtub

Using the rules for brainstorming and the PPC method of evaluating, Uarco's Steve Diller shared with us one far-out exercise he conducted with Uarco's sales team to unleash their creative juices. To get things rolling, Steve asked the sales team to break into small groups of five to six people and brainstorm for ten minutes on the following assignment:

Design the perfect bathtub.

After ten minutes of brainstorming, they created some interesting suggestions.

We want to share a few of the best ideas with you. But it's important to keep in mind, no one in the group had any preconceived notions about bathtubs except for their daily experience in bathing or taking showers. Talk about *real* customer perceptions!

1. Peel away liners.
2. Temperature control.
3. Contemporary head rests.
4. Sunken tub to conserve floor space.
5. Padded bottom for comfortable sitting.
6. Digital thermostat for automated tub codes to set water levels, temperature, and seat size.
7. Built-in tanning lights.
8. Body-conforming tub shape.
9. Clap-on water controls.
10. Inverted spigots for child protection.

The V-I-S-I-O-N Method in Action

One of the more innovative approaches Uarco took with its problem-solving process was to make this part of its quality effort an interesting exercise. A number of employee teams were created from various departments. Next, each team selected a problem worthy of tackling and, using the V-I-S-I-O-N method, worked the problem through to its successful conclusion. Some teams were more successful than others. But the purpose of the exercise was to demonstrate how the V-I-S-I-O-N method worked and could be applied to solve real problems. Here is an example of the V-I-S-I-O-N method at work.

An accounting department team, named The Reconcilers selected a thorny issue for their project. Their issue was "Errors on Expense Reports Which Slows the Processing Time."

The Reconcilers' problem-solving worksheet is shown in Figure 7-2 on page 189. As you will see, their first step was to *visualize the problem:* A majority of submitted expense reports contain inaccurate or insufficient information, which causes delays in processing and reimbursement of expense reports at the general office.

As you examine Figures 7-3 on page 190 and 7-4 on page 191, you will see there were a number of causes listed. These causes were based on a sample of 350 expense reports. The leading culprits were

1. Wrong trip dates.

2. No trip date.

3. No employee number.

4. Insufficient receipts.

5. Math errors.

The Reconcilers' second step was to *identify the baseline.* They calculated that the average time of each defect cost them five minutes. This included callbacks, leaving messages, returning the expense form to the employee for more information, and so on. They also established that the overall defect rate was 26 percent; they set a goal to cut that rate in half.

When The Reconcilers *strategized and planned their solution,* they figured the best solution was to redesign their own form and communicate the most common errors through total quality meetings.

Next, The Reconcilers *implemented* their solution. Responsibilities were assigned along with a time line. Members of the team set out to track daily defects for improvements, expedite new expense report design, and create a tracking report for employees to use as a guideline. (See Figure 7-5 on page 192.)

Problem Solving Worksheet

☒ General Office ☐ Plant_____ ☐ Sales ☐ Other_____	Department/District 　　Accounting	Team Name 　　The Reconcilers	Team Captain 　　Chris Fulk
	Problem 　Errors on Expense Reports Slowing Processing Time		Date 　5/30/91

Visualize Problem	Problem Definition: A majority of submitted expense reports contain inaccurate or insufficient information which causes delays in processing and reimbursement of expense reports at the general office.	Causes: 　(Based on sample of 350 expense reports) 1. Wrong trip dates 2. No trip date 3. No employee number 4. Insufficient receipts 5. Math errors NOTE: • 39% of total causes do not affect processing time • 4% of reports were clean

Identify Base Line	How Much:　(TIME) • Average processing time of each defect is 5 minutes. 　i.e. call, leave message, send back, etc.	How Often: |	# of Defects	% Defect Rate
1.	32	9%
2.	90	26%
3.	63	18%
4.	11	3%
5.	4	1%		How Long: 1 Month (May)
---	---	---	---

Strategize and Plan Solutions	Potential Solutions: 1. Communicate problem through memo 2. Personally explain problem as it arises 3. Follow-up with phone calls 4. Re-design the expense report 5. Send all inaccurate forms back to owner ⁝ 29. Communicate problem through Total Quality Awareness meeting	Best Solution: Combination of: #4. Re-design the form #29. Communicate problem through the Total Quality meetings

Implement Solutions	Responsibilities: • Track daily defects for improvements • Expedite new expense report design • Create example expense report	Time Line: | Start Date:	Finish Date:
June 3	October 31
May 30	June 7
June 7	June 14		Commitment: • Donna Moroz • Tom Looman • Chris Fulk
---	---	---	---

Organize Evaluation Method	Data Display: ☒ Bar Graph ☐ Line Graph ☒ Pie Chart ☒ Pareto Chart ☐ Other	2⊞ Goal: Twice the quality by reducing defects by half	Target: Reduce missing trip date defect from 26% to 13%

Note Results	Measurement Dates: June-October 1991	Results: Reduced defect rate from 26% to 12%	New Base Line: 12% defect rate for missing trip date

CE 284 (5/91) SKU 960815

Your efforts will enable UARCO to better serve our customers.

Figure 7-2　Problem-Solving Worksheet
Source: Uarco Inc.

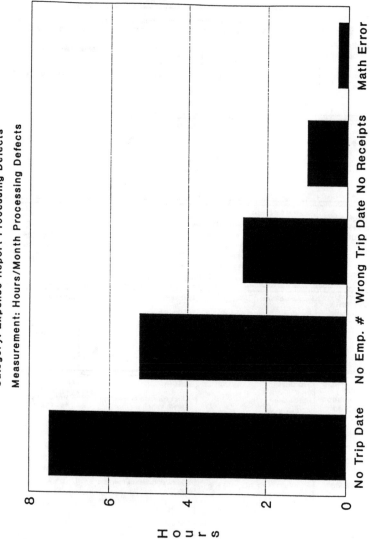

Pareto Chart

Category: Expense Report Processing Defects

Measurement: Hours/Month Processing Defects

No Trip Date   No Emp. #   Wrong Trip Date   No Receipts   Math Error

Based On: Avg. Proc. Time Each Defect = 5 min.

H o u r s

Figure 7-3   Pareto Chart

Source: Uarco Inc.

PIE CHART

Category: Expense Report Processing Defects
Measurement: Defect Rate

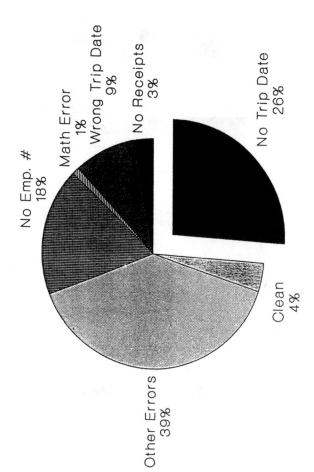

No Emp. #
18%

Math Error
1%
Wrong Trip Date
9%

No Receipts
3%

No Trip Date
26%

Clean
4%

Other Errors
39%

$$\frac{(\text{\# of Defects/Month})}{(\text{\# of Exp. Reports/Month})}$$

Figure 7-4 Pie Chart
Source: Uarco Inc.

191

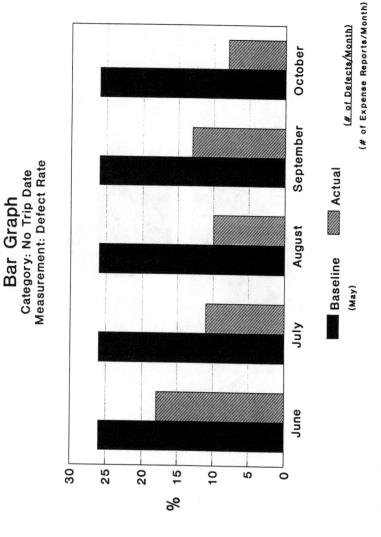

Figure 7-5 Bar Graph
Source: Uarco Inc.

After this was completed, The Reconcilers *organized evaluation methods*. They created bar graphs, pie charts, and a Pareto chart.

Their last step was to *note the results*. Their measurement period was six months. They exceeded their goal by 1 percent.

There's no question that the problem-solving methods Uarco adopted and implemented have helped them on their road to total quality. We encourage you to put into practice these simple, but very worthwhile, methods to improve your overall quality performance.

▼ CADILLAC MOTOR CAR COMPANY (DETROIT, MICHIGAN)

The story of Cadillac is a lesson in cultural change and how to communicate and disseminate values to your employees. It is also the fascinating story of an automotive company that rediscovered success after temporarily letting it slip away. Fortunately, Cadillac got back on the right path by rededicating itself to the very principles on which it was founded in 1902 by Henry Martin Leland.

Cadillac, which derives its name from the French explorer Le Sieur Antoine de la Mothe Cadillac, is the flagship of all General Motors' products. For many decades, Cadillac represented the standard of excellence in American-built automobiles. Cadillac was built on a legacy of superior craftsmanship and unsurpassed quality. Cadillac's first official quality recognition came in 1908 when it was awarded the world-renowned Dewar Trophy—a prize sponsored annually by the Royal Automobile Club of England to encourage technical progress. According to Cadillac's historian, it won the coveted award for its demonstration of the complete interchangeability of parts. This was the first time an American company had received this prestigious award. Cadillac repeated its success by winning the Dewar Trophy in 1915 for its first application of the electric self-starter.

For decades, Cadillac's reputation for quality and innovation went unchallenged. Then, in the 1980s, Cadillac appeared to lose its touch. Radical design changes coupled with a rash of stringent emissions standards and fuel economy requirements caught Cadillac and other American automakers off guard. For the first time in its proud history, Cadillac failed to meet its customers' expectations. Its image was in jeopardy. Other luxury carmakers took advantage of Cadillac's stumble and pounced on its market share with devastating results.

In 1985, after six years of drifting and searching for a comeback, Cadillac turned to a strategy that transformed its culture through quality and customer satisfaction. Five years later, Cadillac's persistence paid off. Cadillac's transformation through its people, systems, processes, and products earned Cadillac the 1990 Malcolm Baldrige National Quality Award, the most prestigious quality award in America.

How did Cadillac transform its culture and make such a dramatic turnaround? The story is an intriguing one because Cadillac uncharacteristically went about its transformation without much fanfare. It was almost too quiet. In fact, several quality experts were so stunned by the announcement that Cadillac had been selected as a Malcolm Baldrige National Quality Award winner that they thought it was a mistake.

Industry studies, including the respected J. D. Power & Associates Survey as well as several automotive industry publications, painted a bleak picture for Cadillac from 1981 to 1985. While Cadillac dealers were rated above average by their customers, Cadillac's product problems abounded. The fit and finish work was lackluster, quality problems surfaced, and product design was booed by loyal Cadillac customers.

When the 1990 Baldrige announcement came, it was a surprise to many General Motors employees. But, regardless of the shock waves, Cadillac deserved the honor after spending five years rebuilding its product quality, its reliability, and customer relationships. As Baldrige insiders have told us, "It is virtually impossible to win this award without earning it. There are too many checks and balances along the way. Whatever Cadillac did, they did enough to catch the eyes of a number of examiners and make a very convincing argument for their continuous improvement processes and commitment to quality and service."

Ironically, that's exactly what Cadillac did in a very unconventional way. Quietly, Cadillac set out in 1987 to reorganize itself into a single business unit. It added engineering and manufacturing to its marketing responsibilities. This decision was made to strengthen the product development emphasis and bring together all the elements necessary to accomplish Cadillac's mission, which is, "to engineer, produce, and market the world's finest automobiles."

This reorganization accomplished several strategic objectives. First, it moved manufacturing and engineering closer to the customer. Second, it gave the people of Cadillac "cradle-to-grave" ownership of the success of our products, and it reinforced in Cadillac employees their commitment to build the world's finest automobiles.

The Cadillac Transformation: Three Key Strategies

What followed was a complete transformation of Cadillac—a transformation that affected the company's processes, products, and services. Cadillac established three strategies behind this transformation:

1. A cultural change
2. A constant focus on the customer
3. A disciplined approach to planning

The highlights of Cadillac's quality story are explained by Steve Seaton, Cadillac's Manager of Service Administration. It is a classic study because it demonstrates what an entrenched, bureaucratic organization can overcome once it makes a commitment to be the best in its class. Cadillac aimed to be the best *in the world!* And, according to recent automotive magazine awards and rankings, Cadillac's 1992 product line has captured numerous awards based on its reemergence as the undisputed customer satisfaction and quality leader among American automobiles.

Cadillac's Cultural Change: Five Ways to Increase Teamwork and Employee Involvement

After several years of sluggish sales and disappointing customer feedback, Cadillac realized that to create the world's finest automobiles, it had to initiate a cultural change. At the heart of this cultural change were teamwork and employee involvement. Cadillac identified five initiatives that were primarily responsible for increasing teamwork and employee involvement. They are:

1. Simultaneous engineering

2. Supplier partnerships

3. The UAW-GM quality network

4. Cadillac people

5. Cadillac's relationship with its dealers

1. Simultaneous Engineering

In 1985, simultaneous engineering became the key strategy for Cadillac's product development and improvement process. (*Simultaneous engineering* is defined by Cadillac as "a process in which appropriate disciplines are committed to work interactively to conceive, approve, develop, and implement product programs that meet predetermined Cadillac objectives.")

Cadillac developed a pyramid to depict its simultaneous engineering structure. (See Figure 7-6.) It is supported by Cadillac's executive staff and the Simultaneous Engineering Steering Committee, leadership groups that nurture the process and allocate resources. They support the Vehicle Teams, Vehicle System Management Teams, and Product Development and Improvement Teams. These teams are responsible for the quality, cost, timing, and technology of Cadillac vehicles, systems, and components. In turn, the teams support the operators in the plants, who support Cadillac's dealers and customers.

Cadillac knew that extensive teamwork was necessary to break down the communication barriers and walls that prevented cross-team cooperation. In 1992, simultaneous engineering teams involved nearly

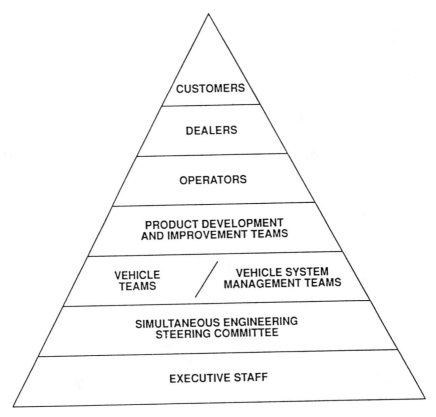

Figure 7-6 The Simultaneous Engineering Pyramid
Source: Cadillac

700 employees—including suppliers and dealers—who were responsible for defining, engineering, marketing, and continuously improving all Cadillac vehicles.

Product design and development now begins with integrated knowledge of all key success factors. This leads to better decisions and the ability to get to market more quickly with automobiles that are on target.

2. Supplier Partnerships

Simultaneous engineering would not be possible without the close working relationship of Cadillac's suppliers. In 1985, Cadillac began the tedious process of redefining its supplier relationships by asking suppliers to take on additional product development responsibilities. This effort, along with the objective to reduce variation, led to a reduction in the supply base. This allowed a closer, more focused relationship with suppliers.

Cadillac also took a lead role in institutionalizing continuous improvements at supplier locations by participating in GM's "Targets for Excellence" program. Cadillac also set out to build a stronger sense of trust and commitment among its suppliers by regularly scheduling "Partners in Excellence" conferences where key suppliers participated with Cadillac leaders in strategic planning efforts.

3. UAW-GM Quality Network

In 1973, GM and the United Auto Workers began to work together to jointly improve product quality and the quality of work life. In 1987, GM's management and the UAW recognized that a consistent, joint quality improvement process was needed to improve competitiveness. They established the UAW-GM Quality Network, which comprises union and management quality councils at the corporate, group, division, and plant levels. The Quality Network's primary objective is to keep everyone focused on customer satisfaction.

4. The Cadillac People Strategy

Cadillac realized that to regain its market lead and achieve total quality, the success of its efforts would depend on its people. The Cadillac People Strategy was designed to meet the needs of Cadillac people while achieving the goals of the company's business plan. The backbone of this strategy was to empower employees to take responsibility for making quality a reality. At the same time, management made a concerted effort to earn the trust of Cadillac's employees.

Cadillac determined that the key to its people strategy was in its selection/hiring process. Second, efforts had to be made to place people in positions where their talents could best be utilized. Third, Cadillac wanted to develop its people and grow them so that they would actively participate in the decision-making process. Communication channels had to be created so that a dialogue was started and ideas were freely exchanged. Finally, rewards and recognition programs were created to support the behaviors necessary to achieve Cadillac's business plan. In the final analysis, Cadillac's management had to stop treating its UAW employees primarily as "union people" and, instead, transform them into "Cadillac people." This was a major transition for Cadillac—a difficult feat for an entrenched unionized company.

5. Cadillac's Dealer Relationships

To integrate fully all the players into the teamwork culture, a new partnership was forged with Cadillac's dealers. Today, Cadillac's dealers, through the National Dealers Council and other sources, are brought into the decision-making process on everything from new products and advertising to operating policies. Their opinions are solicited and, more important, given serious consideration prior to the final verdict being reached. This represents a sharp departure—but positive move—from the "old way" Cadillac used to do business.

Focusing on the Cadillac Customer

Cadillac realized that customer satisfaction *was* the master plan. If customers were no longer satisfied with the product, nothing else mattered. So Cadillac began to redefine its culture and break down the walls between functions and allowed people to focus on their internal and external customers.

According to Cadillac, the company's focus on internal customers centers on its design for manufacturability strategy which gives its engineering teams a disciplined approach for considering manufacturing requirements throughout the entire product development process. The net result of these team efforts was the creation of an innovative manufacturing process called assembly line effectiveness center (ALEC), which is a simulated manufacturing environment used to evaluate the "buildability" of future models. At ALEC, the voice of the assembler is captured much earlier in the design and building process. This translates to a better product at less cost and an expedited cycle time.

Instituting Change

In the past few years, as a result of Cadillac's recommitment to quality, several customer service programs have been instituted:

CADSTAR. This provides Cadillac dealer service technicians with comprehensive, up-to-date service information and procedures.

Cadillac Roadside Service. This program is available to all Cadillac owners regardless of the model or year of their car. This round-the-clock service is available through a toll-free telephone number 24 hours a day, 365 days per year. Trained service advisors or technicians assist owners by either walking them through a repair or dispatching a roadside assistance vehicle from the closest Cadillac dealership.

Cadillac Gold Key Courtesy Transportation. The Gold Key Plan makes alternative transportation available to any Cadillac customer whose vehicle is brought in for warranty repairs. It includes loaner vehicles when the repair requires that an owner's Cadillac be kept at the dealership overnight.

Cadillac Consumer Relations Center. This center is accessed through a toll-free number where professionally trained representatives respond immediately to the questions and concerns of Cadillac customers and potential customers. The center utilizes case tracking systems to create management reports that are analyzed and distributed to simultaneous engineering teams and customer satisfaction personnel.

In addition to these customer service programs, Cadillac increased its product warranty coverage to four years or 50,000 miles without a deductible payment.

Cadillac's Four Planning Objectives

As we've mentioned, at Cadillac, its business plan is the quality plan. The thrust of its business plan has four objectives:

1. To involve every employee in the running of the business
2. To continually reinforce Cadillac's mission and long-term strategic objectives throughout the organization
3. To align the shorter-term business objectives with the goals and action plans developed by every plant and functional staff
4. To institutionalize continuous improvement of our products and services

To ensure that these objectives were met, Cadillac asks each plant to develop a quality plan that aligns its respective goals with the company's overall business plan. Each year, every employee receives a detailed brochure of the business plan, which is known as *Aligning the Arrows*. This brochure addresses the components of Cadillac's quality plan. Those areas are mission, strategic objectives, business objectives, goals, and action plans.

The bottom-line results at Cadillac have been considerable. As a direct result of its move to a team-based culture, a renewed focus on the customer, and a disciplined approach to planning, Cadillac has registered impressive gains with its products, processes, and service measures. One measurement tool, GM's customer-oriented vehicle evaluation (COVE), is a combined static (stationary and dynamic [driven]) vehicle audit conducted on finished vehicles awaiting shipment. From 1986 to 1991, Cadillac's entire product line has improved on this measure by 55 percent and is competitive with world-class products.

Another measurement area which Cadillac has emphasized is reliability and durability. Cadillac understands that these two areas have a significant impact on customer purchase and repurchase considerations.

GM developed a comprehensive testing program to predict the number of "things gone wrong" at 50,000 test miles. This equates to 100,000 customer-driven miles and ten years of exposure to the natural elements. This test is conducted on all vehicles throughout the product development process and continues after the car is in production. By 1991, Cadillac's combined product line in this area had improved 67 percent since 1986 to levels at or exceeding world-class performance!

Measuring the Process Quality Improvements

In addition to product quality improvements, Cadillac's product development process and total quality culture have led to a significant improvement in process quality measures. Here are a few examples Cadillac shared with the Baldrige Award examiners:

1. In stamping plants, operational flexibility enables just-in-time delivery of parts and responsiveness to customer requirements. At Cadillac's Grand Blanc facility, tool transition improved 65 percent in just two years.

2. The up-front teamwork and cross-functional cooperation achieved through simultaneous engineering has contributed to a 56 percent reduction since 1985 in the number of engineering changes issued in a model year and a significant reduction in the total lead time required for styling changes and completely new products.

3. Cadillac's efforts to simplify the build process and reduce variation resulted in a 90 percent decrease in build combinations, which reduces variation in the assembly plant.

4. Target build, which is the percentage of cars built in the scheduled week, has improved 67 percent since 1987, and productivity—as measured by assembly hours per car—has improved 58 percent at the Detroit-Hamtramck Assembly Center.

5. The service aspect of the business has also benefited from continuous improvement. The technical assistance hotline provided to

Cadillac dealer service technicians has continuously been rated highest in the corporation with user satisfaction numbers consistently in the 90–100 percent range.

6. Supplier quality measures also show improvement. Since the 1987 implementation of targets for excellence, the number of new production parts approved on schedule has increased by 21 percent. The number of suppliers delivering just-in-time has increased by 425 percent since 1986.

The ultimate measure of a company's performance is determined by the customer. Cadillac's recommitment to quality and service has made a major difference to customer satisfaction, product innovations, and the company's overall quality process.

Since Cadillac began its comeback "to engineer, produce, and market the world's finest automobiles" in 1985, overall satisfaction with the product as measured by the GM Customer Satisfaction Index has improved by more than eight points.

Customers' ratings of overall satisfaction with the car after one to five years of ownership as measured by GM's internal surveys had improved 19 percentage points over the last five years. On this measure, Cadillac ranks highest among domestic luxury producers. Satisfaction with service has improved 8 percentage points. And, Cadillac's rating of the total ownership experience has improved 13 percent over the past five years.

Cadillac has also earned increasing respect among domestic car buyers. For five years in a row (1987–1991), Cadillac was ranked as the number one domestic make on the independent J. D. Power & Associates Customer Satisfaction Index, improving 42 percent since 1986.

Finally, Cadillac's repurchase loyalty has made a 24 percent improvement in the last three years and now represents the best in the domestic car industry.

In a word, Cadillac is an example of the *positive* results a company can realize once it makes a *commitment* to be the best-in-its-class.

▼ BALBOA TRAVEL, INC. (SAN DIEGO, CALIFORNIA)

In 1969, a brother and sister believed that the state of California was on a fast-growth track that would present an opportunity for a top-flight travel agency. So they purchased a small hometown travel operation. Twenty-two years later Jose (Joe) da Rosa and his sister Mary Alice Gonsalves manage Balboa Travel, Inc., the largest travel agency in San Diego. Currently, Balboa Travel operates eight locations with 110 employees. And offices reach from San Diego to San Francisco, with satellite ticket facilities in Washington, DC. Balboa Travel's yearly sales recently hit the $55 million mark.

Balboa Travel operates two different business groups: Travel and Incentives & Motivation. The Travel Division handles the retail travel agency business, including corporate, government, and group travel. Bill Best, Senior Vice President, an experienced travel professional, oversees this operation. The Incentive & Motivation Division handles primarily corporate incentive programs.

The Keys to Balboa's Quality Success: Relationship Building and Profitability

Balboa Travel attributes its success to two of the basic tenets of total quality: relationship building and profitability. Many of Balboa Travel's best customers attribute their long-term relationship with the company to the special attention Balboa's employees provide them. This high level of commitment recently earned Balboa Travel the prestigious award from The World Trade Association of San Diego, Inc., as its "Service Company of the Year."

In the past, travel agencies were buried in paper, did everything manually, and the telephone was the only way to place reservations. This was also a period when every agency did everything—there were few specialists and business travelers seldom received special attention. More often than not, unless the agency was strategically located in a downtown area or busy intersection, attracting new customers was a challenge.

Today, with electronic mail, sophisticated reservations systems, and state-of-the-art back-office support, agencies like Balboa Travel are now professional travel management organizations. Add to this the robotic software which provides multiple quality checks like lowest fares, preferred seats, special meals, etc. But, nothing will replace the personal attention of an experienced Travel Counselor.

This is one reason why the careful selection of customer-friendly employees is crucial to the success of a service-driven company like Balboa Travel. An outstanding travel agent must not only possess a strong knowledge base, but also must have superb telephone skills and the time management skills required to respond to hundreds of varied clients daily. Their telephone mannerisms, friendly voices, and "can-do" attitudes are the characteristics Balboa Travel's managers look for whenever hiring new employees. It is this good-natured, but professional dimension, that has helped Balboa Travel maintain its high level of customer satisfaction.

Three Factors for Balboa's Quality of Service

In our discussions we learned that the quality of service at Balboa Travel hinges on three factors:

1. Superbly-trained employees who are empowered to make decisions on behalf of their clients.

2. Well-educated customers who understand the company's services.

3. Continuous client contact to always be in a position to respond to clients and meet or exceed their expectations.

Client response is one way a travel agency can measure its customer satisfaction levels. Joe da Rosa told us, "The most important message we can send our clients is: 'How fast do we respond?' We view our response time as an important indicator of client satisfaction. This is why we've resisted the mega-business syndrome in favor of remaining a strong regional business."

Another factor da Rosa points to that impacts a small company is "the availability of leadership to respond to a customer—leaders absolutely must be in touch with customers."

Implementing a "Can Do" Culture on Monday Morning

At Balboa Travel, Joe da Rosa and Mary Alice Gonsalves spend much of their time infusing two very basic business tenets into daily action. First, pay attention to your customers. Second, value your fellow employees and what they do. Help them succeed.

Paying attention to their own shortcomings is another element of Balboa's success. Management examines and investigates every customer response card and tries to get to the bottom of "why the customer was pleased or displeased" with Balboa's service or the overall travel experience. Balboa's customer relations manager has been trained to focus on the entire relationship with the customer.

Every morning Balboa Travel's senior managers review industry trends. "We've always paid attention to what's coming around the bend," da Rosa told us. He added, "Balboa Travel realized early on that its better to be ahead of the train than lying down on the tracks. This is what has taken us to the next level, and then the next, etc."

In our research of best-in-class companies, we have found that this leadership style or approach to communicating and acting on its business philosophy can become infectious. When a company's leadership acts, employees take note of the way their leaders made a decision, or pondered the decision-making process, and arrived at their decision. Invariably, employees down the line begin to think and act on that same level and assume greater responsibility and risks in a spontaneous way.

The Power of Positive Communication

Another strength of Balboa Travel's management team is their communication skills. "One of the things we pay attention to," according to

Senior Vice President Bill Best, "is our employees' need to know what's going on. This might sound almost elementary, but we've learned that information is strategic. How we use it can give us a competitive edge. It also tells people they're important. The process of conveying information helps people feel good about themselves and keeps them in the know. We place a high importance on exchanging information at our manager meetings, and we expect our managers to communicate even the most trivial information to their associates."

Best described how the communication flow process benefits Balboa Travel. He said, "One suggestion our employees came up with in order to keep everybody in the loop was a staff newsletter. We also rely heavily on inner-branch E-mail so there is a constant free flow of messages back and forth. When a company is spread out across the map like we are, you can't call everybody together into the lunch room and tell them what's going on."

The concept of "shared successes" is another dimension of Balboa Travel's business success. "We understand and appreciate that our employees work long hours," says da Rosa. He adds, "being a travel agent or a support person in this company is a very demanding job. It requires stamina to stay on the phone, project confidence, and remain upbeat. So this is why we believe in sharing our success. When we make money, every employee shares in the profits. Everyone plays a strategic role in Balboa Travel's success, and we always try to drive home the message that 'you count, you do make a difference.'"

Finding and Keeping the Right People

Another challenge that confronts every small business—including Balboa Travel—is finding and keeping good people. Bill Best said, "We think our people success is due to a three-pronged approach—that is, finding the right people, hiring them, and keeping them."

When it comes to finding people, Balboa believes that success breeds success, so they ask their employees to recommend possible candidates. They also rely on travel institute graduates and always post all job openings. As Best explained, everybody in the company has a shot at any job for which they want to apply.

In terms of hiring the right people, Best believes that management must match the right person with the right job. Noting that every job here requires different skills, once the employee is hired or transferred to a new job, proper training is the key to their success. According to Best, it is management's job to ensure that every employee succeeds. He added, "If someone fails to make it here, it's typically management's fault not the employee's. We have to make time to help that person get oriented and learn as much about the job as quickly as possible. This way, we maintain their interest and enthusiasm, and we ensure they'll succeed and be an asset to our operation."

Keeping good people is always a challenge when you're best-in-class. Other companies and competitors want to hire away your best and brightest. "Put yourself in their shoes," da Rosa told us. "I know I'd want to work for a company that is committed to my professional growth, that cares about my career path, and is willing to invest in me. Beyond that, I want to receive a competitive wage, benefits, and I want a company that is flexible and receptive to my ideas. At Balboa Travel, we have an environment that allows people to make mistakes, to grow professionally from both their successes and failures, and an environment that tells people they are making a difference."

Five Ways to Improve Client Relations

When it comes to client relations, Balboa Travel is at its very best. This is due in part to a deeply rooted belief that its customers are the most important part of their business.

We asked associates at Balboa Travel to share with us some of the ways they relate to their customers. Here is an abbreviated list of Balboa's everyday practices:

- Encourage clients to return the ticket feedback forms/surveys so we know what they liked or disliked about our service and their trip.

- Always be aware of who ultimately pays your salary and why you exist: to serve your customers.

- Make a sincere effort to get close to your clients by educating them on travel matters, meeting with them throughout the year, and including them on appropriate educational trips.

- Make use of "information exchanges" such as travel budgeting seminars and off-site programs for our clients.

Educating Customers

"The best customer is an educated customer," according to da Rosa. He also believes that the first job of a salesperson is to educate the customer. "At Balboa Travel," he told us, "we learned many years ago that the key to keeping customers is to educate them on how best to interact with our industry and work together with us."

Managing Your Profitability

On the profitability side of the ledger, Mary Alice Gonsalves is the keeper of all essential client data. Her methods are more oriented to a professional saleswoman than an accountant or chief financial officer. She said, "Most people don't think numerically. Therefore, we have to leave our accountant mind-set in the office when we prepare reports for our clients. When we review the numbers face to face with a client, they understand it better. Business managers appreciate the fact that we've taken the time to prepare this information for them. Clients like to have a historical performance of their travel and entertainment budgets as well as a biannual client assessment of how they can maximize their travel dollars with us."

The Service Performance Graph for Measuring Progress

To evaluate and measure their progress, Balboa Travel uses the Service Performance Graph. "When it comes to human mistakes, however minimal," da Rosa told us, "the key is to know the *tolerance level* of each and every customer. We work smart and hard to keep mistakes and errors well within the range acceptable to our customers.

The Service Performance Graph (see Figure 7-7) shows that a company can operate with varying degrees of service flexibility provided it stays within the Positive Performance Zone. Once a company attempts to maximize its profits or reduce its service below tolerable levels, it risks stepping out of the Positive Performance Zone line and losing its customers. The Positive Performance Zone area is bordered by the Customer Low Tolerance Area on the left, which represents High Performance but High Costs, and the Customer Lost Area on the right, which represents Unsatisfactory Performance at Any Cost."

"Customer Low Tolerance" Area	*"Positive Performance" Zone*	*"Customer Lost" Area*
High Margins	Reasonable Margins	Very Tight Margins
High Resource Requirement	Partnership for Quality	Limited Resource Commitment
High Service Demand	Service Satisfaction	Service is Shaky
Low Tolerance	Customer Retention	Tolerance Exhausted

Figure 7-7 The Service Performance Graph
Source: Joe da Rosa, Balboa Travel, Inc., San Diego, CA.

The Positive Performance Experience Zone is the maximum area in which companies want to operate—making a sufficient profit and utilizing their employees in a proficient manner. However, whenever a company moves too far left and, eventually, falls out of the Positive Performance Zone by trying to raise its profits or over-taxing its people, or operating systems capabilities (which in turn frustrates customers), the company runs the risk of losing its customers.

Examples of how a company might lose customers by shifting into the Customer Low Tolerance Area include charging too much for the real or perceived value of a premium item such as a premium-priced hotel which does not provide extra amenities or a "luxury" car which is viewed as a midrange product.

An example of how a company might fall into the Customers Lost Area includes a bank that understaffs its drive-up teller windows at peak hours or a retail store that has a very rigid "No Return" policy. According to da Rosa, "One job of management is to keep its company in the Positive Performance Zone."

Balboa Travel is doing a very good job of staying within its Positive Performance Zone. Although the 1990s are proving to be a very challenging decade for the travel industry, Balboa Travel is making its profit and growth goals through its commitment to quality service and personal attention to its customers.

Chapter Eight

How to Lead Your Staff in the Pursuit of Quality

Experience is by industry achieved. And perfected by the swift course of time.

WILLIAM SHAKESPEARE
The Two Gentlemen of Verona

We cannot overemphasize the importance of management's role in creating a quality-driven organization where the pursuit of quality is imbedded in all processes and is more than just a slogan or short-term campaign. Because of the difference in processes from firm to firm, in the final analysis, each company must find its own way.

However, one way we can help is to share with you the thoughts and views of champions who have blazed the trail before us. Although every trail is different and unique to the company that travels it, we recognize that other quality champions have confronted many of the same questions and overcome organizational barriers you are facing. We want to share with you the thoughts of two respected champions.

We spoke recently with Philip C. Lee, a successful entrepreneur in Southern California and founder of The Leader's Edge, a progressive consulting practice dedicated to the professional development of CEOs and other senior executives. In 1970 he founded a destination management firm within the hospitality industry and built it into a multimillion-dollar business. Along the way, Lee groomed a number of his key employees who eventually bought the company's four Southern California locations.

We also spoke with Aleta Holub, one of the quality architects at First Chicago Bank and a Malcolm Baldrige Award judge. Holub has seen the development of quality and service from the perspective of a major financial service corporation. During her tenure at First Chicago, the bank has earned a solid reputation as a best-in-class operation.

Over the past few years, we have had the opportunity to speak with and interview many outstanding quality leaders and champions. We wanted to share our conversations with Phil Lee and Aleta Holub because they truly represent that segment of American business that has struggled with the challenges of creating a quality process and succeeded. One of these individuals hails from a small company; the other from a major financial institution.

Their approaches to quality are different, yet, they are similar in many respects because the basic values and teachings they have applied to achieve quality in their respective companies are surprisingly similar. We invite you to read on and discover from them how you can begin to implement a quality process and teach your people how to live every day in total quality.

▼ PHILIP C. LEE, FOUNDER
The Leader's Edge (San Diego, California)

Authors: What should managers do on Monday morning if they want to create a total quality process in their company?

Lee: I believe the first thing that must happen on Monday morning is that managers must focus on their customers and create a *concern for the customer,* a concern that permeates all levels of the organization.

A manager's first order of business every Monday morning must be *the customer.* And the manager's last order of business every Friday afternoon must be *the customer.* That's what

I mean by *customer focus*, and, frankly, that's what really matters the most, I think.

If your company is starting its management meetings, or sales meetings, or accounting meetings with any other lead agenda item, you're missing the mark and you're wasting your time on secondary items that are not top priorities because they don't concern *the customer*. I call this majoring in the minors. If you think I'm talking nonsense here, just ask your best customer to sit in on one of your power meetings and invite him to tell you what matters most. I've done that, and it was a real shock to learn that my very best customers— those twenty percenters who keep my doors open—they really only cared about things that resulted in better quality, better service, and a better experience for them. Period! That's all that really matters in the final analysis.

Yet, too many managers see it differently and I suppose that's what makes one business a success and another business a failure. I like to draw the analogy of achieving quality to a great hitter in baseball. Have you ever wondered why one ball player has a batting average of .200 and another player, say, Ted Williams, can bat over .400? I've wondered about it and I found out that Ted Williams had better vision and concentration than most ball players. He was able to see the rotation of the baseball as it left the pitcher's hand and came rocketing toward home plate. In other words, Ted Williams kept his eye on the ball, and, as a result, he hit more pitches. And it's as true in business as it is in baseball or any other endeavor. The company that keeps its eye on the ball—the customers—and stays focused with a clear vision is going to have more success.

Authors: Translate that into action on Monday morning.

Lee: Getting back to what to do on Monday morning, I think management has to institute a customer satisfaction process that allows employees to be partners in the quality process and take ownership in achieving higher levels of customer satisfaction. It should be a natural process in the sense that your people want to be involved because it builds their self-esteem and makes them whole as a person. I think L. L. Bean, Nordstrom, and the Ritz-Carlton Hotels have been able to achieve such a process on a consistent basis. But let me give you another example.

I recently returned from an extended trip to Europe. I was impressed by the level of commitment among front-line employees in European stores and shops and the level of service they provided their customers. It wasn't just the shop owners who had this spirit of service, but their employees as well. There were very few times when I walked into a shop and I wasn't immediately welcomed and encouraged to become a *paying* customer. I wasn't pressured either; but rather, it was their subtle way of doing business by building a relationship with people—one at a time—as we entered their shop. They take an interest in people as human beings and make them feel special.

Personalized Service: The Missing Ingredient

Authors: Why are we often missing this dimension of personalized service in the United States?

Lee: Perhaps it's a cultural issue. Many Europeans and the Japanese have far less tolerance for poor service. It is contrary to their cultures. But in the United States, more often than not, we're pleasantly surprised to walk into a store, hotel, or manufacturer and find somebody who acknowledges our presence—let alone is prepared to provide outstanding service. I see pockets of excellence throughout the Midwest and South in smaller towns as well as in many family-owned businesses because across America there's a pride factor among them. But, for the most part, I think American companies are falling short in providing a memorable service experience to their customers. We're very inconsistent.

The Role of Management in Restructuring the Company's Approach to Quality

Authors: So what role does management play in restructuring their company's approach to quality and service?

Lee: American management has to start filling the holes and shoring up this kind of mediocre service performance by both management and employees. And I don't necessarily hold the employees accountable because I've learned that employees—for the most part—follow management's lead. If the fish stinks, it usually stinks from the head down. So management is the real culprit here, not the employees. Management must start to lead by example and walk their own talk.

Changing the negative service attitude and culture in America is going to be a very tough assignment because serving people doesn't come naturally to Americans in the same way that it does to the Japanese or Europeans. We equate service with *servitude*—that is slavery—as if its beneath us to serve others. We need to break out of this mentality and realize that service to another human being is the greatest gift we can give to someone. We need to create a more supportive, caring, and compassionate attitude within our companies.

Authors: Which comes first in your opinion? Hiring the smile or training the skill?

Lee: Certainly educating and training employees is one way to improve quality and overall service performance. But the tough thing is that you cannot legislate *caring* for people. When you hire someone, that individual either cares about people or he doesn't. If you're operating a service-driven business, you had better make sure everybody in your company *likes* people. Because if they don't like people, they will drive out your customers.

One way I found to help employees take a greater interest in customer service and quality management was by making them stockholders in my company. I sold my company after twenty-two years to my employees in four separate regions. It took me a long time to realize that the only way my employees would make a total commitment to quality and service was by making them stockholders—not necessarily owners—but true stockholders in my company. Once they had a vested interest in the profitability of the business, I knew they would climb any mountain, overcome any problem to get the job done. And they did just that, year after year.

Authors: People are as different as night and day. What can be done with those dedicated individuals who are interested in continuous improvement but might not be "people-persons"?

Lee: I believe that continuous improvement is a mind-set. Customer consciousness is also a mind-set. Either your managers are aware of what needs to be done to satisfy their customers—and they do it—or management is out of touch and too far removed from the customer process. I've learned that some employees just cannot relate on this level of quality and customer care. This doesn't necessarily mean that they should be fired. But it does mean that management failed in the selection process and needs to find a way to remove these employees from direct customer contact jobs and help them find a position that is better suited for their particular style somewhere else in the company.

Over the years, I watched managers come on board and hire other people just like them. It's too bad because a manager only compounds his weaknesses by hiring employees who are just like him. We need to do a better job of helping managers build their self-esteem by surrounding themselves with individuals who can help them grow. This is why I'm a strong believer in feedback systems and measurements.

Facts are friendly. We owe it to our people to let them know how they're doing. Not just once a year but often. If senior management puts in place feedback mechanisms such as frequent performance evaluations and goal setting conferences, a manager is more likely to stay focused on results rather than worrying about pleasing the boss and kow-towing to the conventional wisdom. Feedback must be cherished, not tolerated. Feedback is a tool, not a club.

Authors: What is the customer's role in helping a company achieve quality?

Lee: We talked earlier about education and how a company can educate and train its people. My response is that the customer is our best teacher. Given the chance, the customer will always teach us how to do it right. All we need to do is *listen*. And sometimes that's difficult to do because the *toughest* customers—those men and women who are the most demanding and least diplomatic—are the *best* teachers. Easy customers, on the other hand, are only average teachers. They hold back because they don't want to hurt our feelings or burn bridges. The tough customers believe facts are friendly and so they just hit us over the head with the facts and don't worry about bruised egos.

There are so many ways to train your people. For example, internships, stewardship programs, apprenticeships, mentoring, and so on. They all work. It's just a matter of which works best in your particular environment. But you must be prepared for some resistance to any training program because it requires people to *change*, and it's human nature to resist change at first.

The challenge is to get your people emotionally connected to total quality so that they take ownership and begin to steer the process. Also, I see a movement away from terms such as "training" and "education" and more toward terms like "professional development." People are more inclined to participate seriously in their own professional development, but less inclined to get involved in education and training. I think the hang-up stems from the failure of our educational system to make learning fun and interesting. So you have to acknowledge this fact and try a different approach.

Authors: You've been a strong advocate of champions. Tell us your thoughts about the champion's role in helping a company achieve quality.

Lee: The *role of champions* and the struggles they face in transforming their companies into quality-driven and service-driven entities is a very real issue. Champions are change agents because they force an organization to examine itself and progress.

Unfortunately, I've seen too many companies that are stuck in neutral because they aren't interested in paying the price required to change from whatever they are to what they could be. Usually, it's because they are controlled by old-thinkers who simply don't want to change or don't know how to take that first step toward quality and championing change. They are comfortable with the status quo and are out of touch with their customers and employees. It's understandable, but inexcusable.

What happens to so many dedicated champions who work in this kind of environment is very frustrating. It zaps their energy and stifles their commitment. The kind of change we've been talking about here requires a *real champion at the senior level* who wants his or her legacy to be: "I stirred the pot and got things moving and made a difference in this organization." While a manager-champion is going to encounter a lot of lip service from other managers, he has the authority and power to force change.

The challenge every champion must confront is that most people really don't want change. They just want to survive another few years until they can retire and enjoy the good life. So they sidestep the quality champions by paying lip service to the cause and tell their manager, "Yeah, it sounds great. Go for it." But really they do nothing. Eventually, if the quality champion has no support at the top or has little authority, he either becomes disenchanted and quits or is relegated to a nonthreatening role. That's the down side of this championing business. The only way to counter this successfully is to make sure you have buy in at the top levels and your senior executives really push it—and I mean push it hard. That's what you do on Monday morning to get a quality initiative launched.

On the positive side, I think the most successful companies are those that foster champions at all levels and empower them to do whatever is necessary to improve the quality and service performance. A company that embraces its champions rather than avoids them will always excel. This kind of organization doesn't fear change, it embraces it. A company that encourages its champions to move forward is bound to succeed because its culture and values are sound. For a company or organization to try and foster champions without having a solid culture and proven value system is foolish. There is no way a champion will succeed against such odds.

In my work now, I encourage managers to examine their company's culture and value system to determine whether or not it will sustain change and foster growth.

Authors: How do rewards and recognition factor into the quality process?

Lee: We need to realize that total quality and, ultimately, customer satisfaction is about *nurturing* people and their feelings. I don't think it has as much to do with training or rewarding behavior as it does with valuing other human beings. And I don't know if that can be taught except by living through the principles you embrace and the examples you set.

Managers should stop rewarding people for what is *expected* of them and, instead, start measuring their performance and giving them positive feedback on their successes and failures. I think measuring performance is part of the implied contract when a person is hired.

Let's start rewarding our people for the things they do *above and beyond the call of duty*. I think you call it the "ABCDs of Customer Service." This is what *accountability* is all about. I think we've come full circle because what has to happen on Monday morning is people need to be held *accountable* for what they did last week and what they say they'll do this week.

Managers simply need to make sure that whatever is done makes a difference to their customers and the quality of service customers expect and deserve. Let me add that I like the concept of rewarding people not only for results, but also for progress. Send a message that effort counts, that results are attained by progress and continuous improvement. I think it's wonderful to get it right the first time, but the truth is, most of us don't get it right the first time. So we need to reward progress as well as the right results.

▼ ALETA HOLUB, Vice President, Quality Manager The First National Bank of Chicago (Chicago, Illinois)

The following are excerpts from an interview with Aleta Holub, who spoke with us about the importance of quality and how to stratify your customer base:

Authors: Aleta, you've been pursuing quality at First Chicago Bank for several years. Tell us, what are the primary challenges a quality champion must overcome to succeed?

Holub: The *pursuit of quality* presents a difficult challenge to most companies and their quality champions. What we're talking about from the outset is: How do you turn customers' expectations—and, subsequently, delivering products and services that meet their expectations—into profitable outcomes? I raise the question because whenever you consistently meet the customer's expectations, you also raise the bar a notch or two. Meeting those new levels of customer expectations must also equate to more market share or more customer loyalty, which, in turn, translates to greater profitability.

When you talk about changing the focus and culture of a company to be a quality-driven operation, you have to examine long and hard the consequences of that choice. For example, in our bank we pride ourselves as being a leader in the area of cash management. Our customers expect great service from First Chicago in this area because we have built our reputation as a recognized leader in cash management. But, whenever we slip in the eyes of a customer, we can't just tell the customer, "Well, gosh, we're still better than the ABC Bank or the XYZ Bank!" Our customer won't buy that line. He or she will say, "I know the ABC and XYZ banks don't perform at your level—that's why I'm using you! But we never expected First Chicago *not* to perform at its *reputation level.*"

And so the challenge we face is to compete with other banks that are getting a share of the cash management business by charging the *same price* as First Chicago, but providing a *lesser* quality of service. We must ask ourselves, "Are we forfeiting increased market share and profitability by having to charge the same competitive price, but delivering a higher (more costly) degree of service?"

Authors: Aren't other industry leaders faced with a similar challenge?

Holub: Other outstanding companies are faced with the same challenge as First Chicago. Consider a successful retailer whose reputation is predicated on outstanding service. In many areas they can charge a premium for their products, but people will pay it so long as the quality and outstanding service is there. Customers will tell you that they like the retailer's clothes, their employees, and their return policy. What the retailer is banking on is that their commitment to quality and superior customer service will translate into greater customer loyalty and, in turn, higher revenues or profits for the company. It boils down to the customer deciding to buy his or her sweater at this one retailer instead of another department store—even if that other department store has it on sale—because when they buy it at their favorite retailer, the customer is going to experience all these other *feel good things* that create a "loyal customer." This is what I mean by *raising the service expectation* a notch or two. And a quality-driven company expects that kind of return on their investment when they commit to a *quality-driven approach.* Otherwise, why make the transition?

Authors: Do you think this is why so many American companies have not yet joined the quality movement?

Holub: What we're getting into here has as much to do with quality and service as it does with creating a perception in the mind of your customers that the experience of doing business with your company is worth paying more money. And this is a very tough challenge for service-oriented companies. I think part of the answer may be in educating your employees on value-price ratios so that your customer is willing to pay more for added-value service. Your employees need to understand how this added-value service can benefit the customer and why it may be worth more to them.

For example, a manufacturing company's sales rep can say to a customer, "This is our basic model at $100. But if you want it to do cartwheels, well then, you want our AA model, and that costs $125. And if you want all the bells and whistles, well then the AAA will cost $150!"

But in the service sector, the customer isn't always thinking on that level. They don't view service in terms of value-price ratios.

They think "if one bank can provide great service, why can't all of them? They all should!" So, when they walk into the XYZ Bank and have a positive service experience, they want to know why they should spend *more money* doing business with another bank to get the same level of service. They don't see—nor do they have an understanding of—what goes into creating consistently excellent service. As a country, we've done a poor job in educating our customers in the value of excellent service.

Authors: It sounds like the dilemma Disney has created for the theme park industry.

Holub: Yes, exactly. It's like the customer who walks into a Nordstrom and experiences great service and then walks across the street to a competitor's department store and has to wait in line to have his or her credit checked. Or he or she can't find a salesperson to ring up his or her purchase. It's frustrating, and it causes the customer to wonder, "Why can't this department store perform like Nordstrom?" The fact is, they could, but they don't think or act like Nordstrom. They're not customer focused or quality driven.

A challenge we all face is finding some way to stratify our levels of service so that we can increase the *quality of our service* versus what our competition provides and charges. Hopefully, in our case, the corporate treasurer at ABC Company is willing to pay First Chicago more money because the corporate treasurer perceives a greater value for our services.

Authors: Can you share an example of stratifying service levels?

Holub: An example of how some businesses can stratify their service levels is *hotel rooms.* A hotel may charge $250 for an ocean view sleeping room versus $200 for a room without an ocean view. I think it's going to be a real struggle for service-driven companies to figure out how they consistently ensure a quality experience for their customers and still have a tiered-level of quality that the customer is willing to pay for above and beyond the basic level.

So this is one of the more critical challenges we face in the service sector. With a few exceptions, I don't think service companies have learned how to stratify their services as well as the manufacturers have done.

Authors: How does a company measure the cost of implementing a quality process?

Holub: Part of the problem every company faces in committing to a quality-driven process is factoring the cost of it. I can't say what another bank or service company will spend because each company's formula is different. The factors are different. There is no set answer or price tag. But I do know that whatever we've spent on our quality process, we've received a hefty return on that investment. For example, we know that we can send a money transfer correctly for less than $10. But when we do it incorrectly, it can costs us upwards of $500. So we can invest that $490 savings in prevention and get a very good return on investment.

I've been blessed with not having to explain every nickel or dollar we've invested in this process because our management team is committed. The real cost isn't defined in terms of dollars or cents; it's defined in terms of blood, sweat, and tears. Our management team weighed the costs of emphasizing quality against our long-term business strategy and felt it was not only worth it, but it made good sense to be recognized as a best-in-class company. Our reputation is our calling card, and it opens many doors for First Chicago.

▼ THE PATH TO QUALITY

We hope that at this point you have a clearer map to enhancing your quality process. We feel that the essence of these two interviews captures much of what we have said throughout the book. In our final chapter, we will talk about moving ahead and the importance of vision and values.

CHAPTER NINE

Championing Quality: People, Principles, Processes, and Performance

Good enough isn't.

Pacific Bell philosophy

Throughout this book, we have emphasized three recurring themes: first, the importance of having an unshakable faith and commitment to a quality process; second, the importance of truly understanding your customers' requirements and assessing your ability to meet those requirements; and third, the continuing need to communicate and educate your employees in the ways of quality excellence and reward them for their progress and results.

In closing, we want to share several stories and thoughts that reinforce these three themes. In doing so, we hope that these stories and personal observations will give you the added strength and support necessary to sustain you on your quest for quality.

Commitment is the propelling force for achieving quality and, ultimately, success in any endeavor. One aspect of commitment deals with the morale and welfare of your employees. We have no doubt that a quality-driven organization possesses a high morale among employees. This, in turn, can increase both service level and the product quality.

While attending a workshop for the International Military Community Executives Association (IMCEA), we had the pleasure of listen-

231

ing to a speech by Brigadier General Don Smith, who serves at the Pentagon's Personnel Support Policy & Services Directorate. General Smith shared with us a moving story about the importance of a soldier's morale. But we also found his story to be appropriate for quality and service champions. In many respects, Smith's story not only captures the importance of morale in building a customer-focused and quality-driven team, but it also highlights the importance of making a difference. General Don Smith began the story by saying, "In February 1980, I was fortunate to accompany General Bruce C. Clarke on his final visit to Fort Knox, Kentucky, where he was scheduled to speak to the Armor Officer Advanced Course students. He was also to be honored at a special awards banquet where he would receive the gold medallion of the order of St. George, the highest award given by the U.S. Army Armor Association.

"At this event, General Clarke began by asking the audience a question that appeared to be rather parochial: 'What is morale? What makes up soldier morale?' He then proceeded to answer his own question by sharing with us an incident that occurred many years ago during his service as the military's Commander-in-Chief while stationed in the Republic of Korea:

"General Clarke told us, 'Early one Sunday morning, I was out walking around the installation when I bumped into a young congressman who was visiting Korea as part of a congressional delegation. I asked this young congressman why he was up so early and what he was doing out-and-about at such an early hour? The congressman told me that he had been walking around talking to some of the soldiers. He was checking on their morale. I asked the congressman how he was measuring the soldier's morale, and how he was checking on the morale of the troops? The congressman replied, 'I'm talking to the troops asking them about things such as the food in the mess hall, receiving their mail from back home on time, and the service the recreation center is providing them.'

"'I told the congressman that all of the things he had mentioned were very important and, certainly, had an impact on a soldier's morale. But they really aren't what's most important to a soldier's morale. I told our visitor that what's most important to soldier morale are three elements. Number one, knowing you have an important job; number two, knowing you are doing it well; and, number three, knowing that somebody appreciates it. These are the three most important things affecting a soldier's morale.'

"Well, many, many years passed and, frankly, I hadn't given much thought to this chance meeting with that young congressman back in Korea. But one day out of the clear blue, I received a letter from this now former congressman and it read:

Dear General Clarke:

I just wanted to write and remind you of a visit we had many years ago when you were the commanding officer in Korea. I want you to know that I have given a great deal of thought to the subject of morale—especially lately; and after all these years, I now realize that you were quite right. Morale is, indeed, made up of three things: knowing you have an important job; knowing you are doing it well; and knowing that somebody appreciates it.

"The letter was written from the Oval Office of the White House and signed by Gerald R. Ford, President of the United States."

General Clarke's story about the correlation of a soldier's morale to the worth of his job and self-esteem is a message we should take back to our organizations and tell over and over again. Why? Because every employee, every person wants to perform a meaningful job if we will empower him or her to do so, a job that makes a difference, and a job that people admire, respect, and will reward. Morale is an excellent starting point for building your organization's long-term commitment to quality.

Before your "soldiers" will march in support of your company's mission and goals, they must believe in themselves, and they must believe they are valued. Management cannot assume this to be the case; rather, managers must remind their fellow employees of the goal, reinforce their belief and desire to achieve that goal, and ultimately recognize the employees' efforts and results.

▼ MAKING A COMMITMENT TO LEAD THE WAY

Throughout this book we have repeated a central theme: *commitment.* We believe that the key success factor above all others for achieving total quality and superior service is *commitment* to our customers and employees.

And *commitment* starts with a personal conviction to *total quality. The secret to achieving total quality is that we must lead, live, and act in a qualitative way.* If you are in a leadership role, you must be clear about who you are, where you are going, and how you will get there.

As a leader, you must be able to transmute problems into opportunities. This is ultimately achieved by building relationships with people and challenging them to grow beyond their self-imposed limitations. This is what we mean by the word *surpass.* A leader, by definition, brings a certain capability that inspires people in the organization to move forward.

How is a leader measured? One measure is an introspective examination. Each day a leader should ask: "Did I make a difference today?" More than anything else, leaders are paid to *make a difference* in the lives of their people, their customers, and the communities they serve.

One fallacy of leadership thinking is that people will follow our words rather than our actions. Of course, it doesn't work this way. Successful leaders know this to be true. Employees will respond to our deeds more than our rhetoric. This is why the axiom, "actions speak louder than words" rings true. If you are to achieve *total quality leadership* in your organization, you must first create a *total quality leader* within!

Although there are many degrees of leadership, there are three constants extraordinary leaders possess. First, extraordinary leaders tell the truth. Second, they keep their promises. And third, they have confidence and faith in their people.

Martin Kaplan, Executive Vice President for Regional Markets at Pacific Bell, told us that in order to achieve continuous growth and improvement in an organization, "Every manager must start with a degree of faith in his or her people. The toughest challenge is to get people moving in the same direction. Today's successful managers must inspire confidence in their leadership direction. A successful manager must develop a core service ethic and quality values so people can get behind management."

Marty added that in 1984, following the court-ordered divestiture of the Bell System companies, Pacific Bell established its core values and moved quickly to drive company performance and results through *behavior*. To better connect employees with the business direction, Pacific Bell started sharing performance results, including customer satisfaction data, with its employees so everybody knew where they stood. Through the bonus plan, all Pacific Bell employees had a personal financial stake in customer satisfaction. Additionally, salaried employees had a strong pay-for-performance tie to customer service.

Suddenly, the issues of quality service and customer satisfaction were no longer the slogan of the month. Instead of simply being in the business of installing and repairing telephones, employees redefined their goals and objectives to reflect the changing technology and increased competition; customer satisfaction became their goal. They refocused their energies on maintaining Pacific Bell's service edge. Now, nearly ten years later, Marty reports that this quality and service strategy has helped Pacific Bell maintain its competitiveness in the marketplace.

One question people often ask is: "How can we compete more effectively?" We believe that the solution is tied to designing and implementing a total quality process that is premised on long-term customer satisfaction. We translate this to mean a merging of technical competence with the humanistic factors that result in total quality. The ideal total quality process merges a company's technical applications of continuous improvement with constant attention to company culture and relationship building.

While manufacturing companies have generally adapted better than their service company counterparts in applying statistical measurement and continuous improvement methods, service sector companies have excelled in developing the humanistic side of customer satisfaction. But, as we've learned from the winners of the Malcolm Baldrige National Quality Award, real quality is a blend of both principles and work processes. To achieve best-in-class long-term results, both are required.

▼ THE FOUR "SACRED" OBLIGATIONS OF MANAGEMENT

A. Blanton Godfrey, the Chairman and CEO of the respected Juran Institute, maintains that a "quality management system must be built on a solid foundation consisting of strategic quality management, executive leadership, and a continual focus on the customer."

In a 1992 speech to the Global Quality Congress in Singapore, Godfrey told his audience about the philosophy of Hideo Sugiura, the former chairman of the Honda Motor Company. Sugiura believes that management has "four 'sacred' obligations."

The first is a clear vision of where the company is going. This must be stated precisely and communicated to every member of the organization in language he or she understands.

The second is defining clearly the small number of key objectives that must be achieved if the company is to realize its vision.

The third is the translation of the objectives throughout the entire organization so that each person knows how performing his or her job helps the company achieve those objectives.

Last is a fair and honest appraisal so that each and every employee knows how his or her performance has contributed to the organization's efforts to achieve the key objectives coupled with guidance on how the individual can improve his or her performance.

As part of the summary of *Customer-Focused Quality*, we would like to quote from the policy of the 74th American Assembly, which was created in 1950 to illuminate issues on global competitiveness. We are grateful to A. Blanton Godfrey who resurrected this passage and presented it in his speech to the Global Quality Congress. The Assembly's final report stated:

> We have collected some basic principles of what makes a firm competitive, the first of which is quality. Together all these principles are:
>
> *Quality:* This does not mean quality merely to specifications but quality that improves constantly, quality that is characterized by constant innovations that create a loyal customer. It means achieving this attitude from top to bottom, from board room to the factory floor.
>
> *Low Cost:* This does not [occur] instead of quality, but as a result of quality. It may seem cheaper to shove as many products or services out as fast as possible, but if quality is ignored, the cost in rework, scrap, supervision, and, most of all, disappointed customers will be more expensive than any business can bear.
>
> *Customer-Driven:* The customer is part of the process. The business exists not merely to satisfy the customers' needs today but to anticipate their needs of tomorrow.
>
> *Employee Involvement:* The successful business no longer sees employment as a cost of production but as a resource for production. Although job uncertainty will never be eliminated, it must be recognized that long-term commitment of and to workers is at least as important as machinery or technology. Employee involvement in efforts to improve productivity and quality is vital, and they must also be able to share in the gains.
>
> *Continuous Improvement:* This means never being satisfied; not only with the products or services, but with the way the organization makes the goods, distributes, sells, and services them. Innovation is required in all of these activities.
>
> In the end, it is not simply companies, or even countries, which compete—it is entire societies. We believe that a society that advances the opportunities of each of its people will best advance the prospects for all.

Nearly 50 years later, we must focus more than ever on these same issues and concerns. While our universe has changed dramatically and economic power has shifted to a new world order, in many respects the fundamentals to achieving total quality and customer satisfaction remain unchanged. It boils down to the same four elements that have driven quality since the beginning of time—the "Four P's of Quality," namely people, principles, processes, and performance.

We consider total quality improvement to be a process—a process guided by champions and strong leadership and encompassed by all people in the organization. Throughout the book, we have talked about the components of total quality improvement. Let's look at how all this fits together.

While we were determining how we could succinctly capture the fact that quality improvement is not a program but a continuum—a process that continues in a never-ending loop—our friend, Bruce Hayes, Director of the Software Institute at Motorola, showed us a chart that amazingly depicts this on one page. (See Figure 9-1 on page 239.) Hayes really had gotten it right. Not only did he show all the major pieces, he showed them as the continuum, that never-ending process that is required for continuous improvement. We share this model with you; it's a simple check and balance to help ensure that you integrate and continue your improvement actions.

At about the same time that Hayes showed us his model, we were trying to synthesize the process of customer satisfaction measurement and implementation of improvements based on measurement results for use in a brief presentation. What at first seemed impossible resulted in our design of a one-page graphic that follows Hayes's chart. (See Figure 9-2 on page 240.)

But a review of all the quality charts in the world won't lead to customer satisfaction unless you have a true commitment to making it all happen. You must have *a clear vision of who you are, where you are going, and how you will get there.* **And you must have** *values that are in harmony with what your employees and customers want.* If you do not have a commitment to put a sound quality process in place, a clear vision, and sound values, there is little chance that, over the long term, you will succeed in achieving sustained quality improvements.

CONTINUOUS IMPROVEMENT MODEL

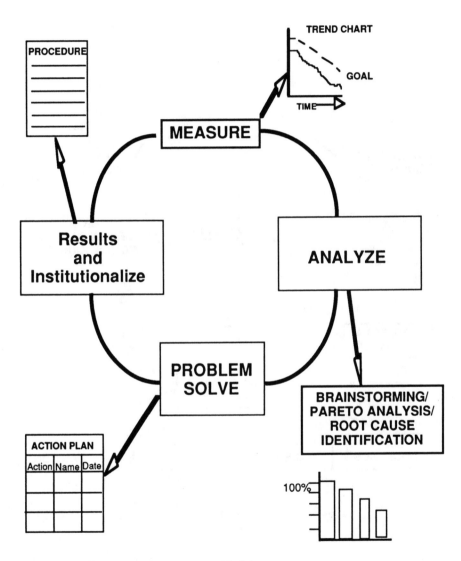

Figure 9-1   Continuous Improvement Model
Source: Bruce Hayes, Motorola

MEASUREMENT PROCESS

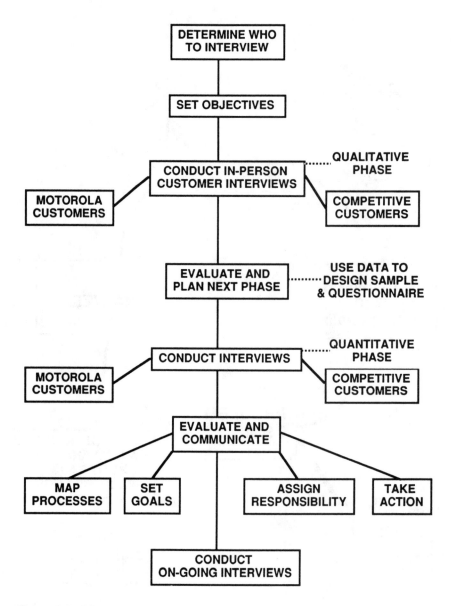

Figure 9-2   Measurement Process

The essence of the previous paragraph is captured on a tiny card to which Motorolans frequently refer. This card summarizes Motorola's beliefs, goals, and initiatives.

▼ MOTOROLA BELIEFS, GOALS, AND INITIATIVES

Key Beliefs—how we will always act

- Constant respect for people
- Uncompromising integrity

Key Goals—what we must accomplish

- Best-in-Class
  - People
  - Marketing
  - Technology
  - Product: Software, Hardware, and Systems
  - Manufacturing
  - Service
- Increased Global Market Share
- Superior Financial Results

Key Initiatives—how we will do it

- Six Sigma Quality
- Total Cycle Time Reduction
- Product, Manufacturing, and Environmental Leadership
- Profit Improvement
- Empowerment for all in a Participative, Cooperative, and Creative Workplace

▼ PUTTING IT ALL TOGETHER

By now, you know there are no simple answers. Best-in-class quality takes a lot of work and diligent effort. But there is a simple phrase that says it all: "Do the right things and do them right."

In his book, *The Macintosh Way,* Guy Kawasaki illustrates the choices we can make. In every business we have four choices. Our choices dictate our consequences. According to Kawasaki, we have four choices. Obviously, doing the *right* thing in the *right* way should always be what you strive for.

Choice 1: Doing the *right* thing the *right* way.

Choice 2: Doing the *right* thing the *wrong* way.

Choice 3: Doing the *wrong* thing the *right* way.

Choice 4: Doing the *wrong* thing the *wrong* way.

Figure 9-3 illustrates these four choices:

	Right Way	Wrong Way
Right Thing	X	
Wrong Thing		

Figure 9-3 Four Choices That Dictate Consequences

To do the *right* things, the right work environment must be established. This is accomplished by your commitment and sustained by goal setting, risk taking, and positive, results-oriented actions. Leaders in an organization determine the quality of the work environment by hiring the right people and giving them the emotional support, resources, and freedom to do their jobs. Remember to empower your employees to do the *right* things. In turn, this ensures their success and your own.

The second half of the equation is doing *things* right. This means paying attention to the details of running your business and building your success brick by brick. Eventually, your people must instinctively learn how to do things right through training and leadership by example. Without strong leadership, your organization cannot succeed.

As a final note, we wish you success in your journey toward total quality. We believe that once you make that first important step of commitment to quality improvement, you will never be able to turn back. This is what customer-focused quality is all about.

APPENDIX ONE

The Malcolm Baldrige Award and Criteria

We've referred to the Baldrige Award throughout this book because it is the one award that best symbolizes the epitome of quality and service excellence among American businesses. For those of you who are not familiar with the details of the Baldrige Award criteria, the following information will provide you with more insight.

The Malcolm Baldrige National Quality Award is administered by the National Institute of Standards Technology (NIST) and the American Society for Quality Control (ASQC). NIST, an agency of the U.S. Department of Commerce, is located in Gaithersburg, Maryland; ASQC is headquartered in Milwaukee, Wisconsin.

The Baldrige Award generates more goodwill for the quality-driven efforts of American businesses than does recognition by any other government agency. And NIST has gained a reputation as one of the most capable and efficient government agencies as a result of its efforts in managing the Baldrige application process.

The Baldrige program is financed by private business and managed as a partnership. Examiners, senior examiners, and judges—collectively known as the Board of Examiners—recommend the winners to NIST and the Secretary of Commerce. These examiners are selected from the ranks of industry, associations, universities, and government agencies. In November of each year, the Baldrige Award is presented by the president of the United States to as many as six winners.

The Baldrige Award emphasizes specific values and concepts. We share with you an interpretation of these values which appeared in a recent Award Criteria; these values are the best examples we have found of a *quality-driven* strategy.

▼ BALDRIGE AWARD CORE CONCEPTS AND VALUES

Customer-Driven Quality

Quality is judged by the customer. All product and service attributes that contribute value to the customer and lead to customer satisfaction and preference must be the foundation for a company's quality system. Value, satisfaction, and preference may be influenced by many factors throughout the customer's overall purchase, ownership, and service experiences. These factors include the company's relationship with customers that helps build trust, confidence, and loyalty. This concept of quality includes not only the product and service attributes that meet basic customer requirements, but it also includes those that enhance them and differentiate them from competing offerings. Such enhancement and differentiation may be based upon new offerings, combinations of product and service offerings, rapid response, or special relationships.

Customer-driven quality is thus a strategic concept. It is directed toward customer retention and market share gain. It demands constant sensitivity to emerging customer and market requirements, and measurement of the factors that drive customer satisfaction and retention. It also demands awareness of developments in technology, and rapid and flexible response to customer and market requirements.

Such requirements extend well beyond defect and error reduction, merely meeting specifications, and reducing complaints. Nevertheless, defect and error reduction and elimination of causes of dissatisfaction contribute significantly to the customers' view of quality and are thus also important parts of customer-driven quality. In addition, the company's success in recovering from defects and errors ("making things right for the customer") is crucial to building customer relationships and to customer retention.

Leadership

A company's senior leaders must create a customer orientation, clear and visible quality values, and high expectations. Reinforcement of the values and expectations requires substantial personal commitment and involvement. The leaders' basic values and commitment need to include areas of public responsibility and corporate citizenship. The leaders must take part in the creation of strategies, systems, and methods for achieving excellence. The systems and methods need to guide all activities and decisions of the company. The senior leaders must commit to the growth and development of the entire work force and should encourage participation and creativity by all employees. Through their regular personal involvement in visible activities, such as planning, communications, review of company quality performance, and recognizing employees for quality achievement, the senior leaders serve as role models reinforcing the values and encouraging leadership in all levels of management.

Continuous Improvement

Achieving the highest levels of quality and competitiveness requires a well-defined and well-executed approach to continuous improvement. The term "continuous improvement" refers to both incremental and "breakthrough" improvement. A focus on improvement needs to be a part of all operations and all work unit activities of a company.

Improvements may be of several types: (1) enhancing value to customers through new and improved products and services; (2) reducing errors, defects, and waste; (3) improving responsiveness and cycle time performance; (4) improving productivity and effectiveness in the use of all resources; and (5) improving the company's performance and leadership position in fulfilling its public responsibilities and serving as a role model in corporate citizenship. Thus, improvement is driven not only by the objective to provide better product and service quality, but also by the need to be responsive and efficient— both conferring additional marketplace advantages. To meet all of these objectives, the process of continuous improvement must contain regular cycles of planning, execution, and evaluation. This requires a basis—preferably a quantitative basis—for assessing progress, and for deriving information for future cycles of improvement. Such information should provide direct links between desired performance and internal operations.

Employee Participation and Development

A company's success in meeting its quality and performance objectives depends increasingly on work force quality and involvement. The close link between employee satisfaction and customer satisfaction creates a "shared fate" relationship between companies and employees. For this reason, employee satisfaction measurement provides an important indicator of the company's efforts to improve customer satisfaction and operating performance. Improving company performance requires improvements at all levels within a company. This, in turn, depends upon the skills and dedication of the entire work force. Companies need to invest in the development of the work force and to seek new avenues to involve employees in problem solving and decision making. Factors that bear upon the safety, health, well-being, and morale of employees need to be part of the company's continuous improvement objectives. Increasingly, training and participation need to be tailored to a more diverse work force, and to more flexible work organizations.

Fast Response

Success in competitive markets increasingly demands ever-shorter cycles for new or improved product and service introduction. Also, faster, and more flexible response to customers is now a more critical requirement of business management. Major improvements in response time often require work organizations, work processes and work paths to be simplified and shortened. To accomplish such improvement more attention should be given to measuring time performance. This can be done by making response time a key indicator for work unit improvement processes. There are other important benefits derived from this focus: response time improvements often drive simultaneous improvements in organization, quality, and productivity. Hence it is beneficial to consider response time, quality and productivity objectives together.

Design Quality and Prevention

Quality systems should place strong emphasis on design quality—problem and waste prevention achieved through building quality into products and services and into the processes through which they are produced. In general, costs of preventing problems at the design stage are much lower than costs of correcting problems which occur "downstream." Design quality includes the creation of fault-tolerant (robust) processes and products.

A major issue in the competitive environment is the design-to-introduction ("product generation") cycle time. Meeting the demands of ever-more rapidly changing markets requires that companies carry out stage-to-stage coordination of functions and activities from basic research to commercialization.

Consistent with the theme of design quality and prevention, continuous improvement and corrective action need to emphasize interventions "upstream"—at early stages in processes. This approach yields the maximum overall benefits of improvements and corrections. Such upstream intervention also needs to take into account the company's suppliers.

Long-Range Outlook

Achieving quality and market leadership requires a company to have a strong future orientation and a willingness to make long-term commitments to customers, employees, suppliers, stockholders, and the community. Planning needs to determine or anticipate many types of changes including those that may affect customers' expectations of products and services, technological developments, changing customer segments, evolving regulatory requirements and community/societal expectations, or thrusts by competitors. Plans, strategies, and resource allocations need to reflect these commitments and changes. A major part of the long-term commitment relates to the development of employees and suppliers, and to fulfilling public responsibilities and serving as a corporate citizenship role model.

Management by Fact

Pursuit of quality and operational performance goals of the company requires that process management be based upon reliable information, data, and analysis. Facts and data needed for quality improvement and quality assessment are of many types, including: customer, product and service performance, operations, market, competitive comparisons, supplier, employee-related, and cost and financial. Analysis refers to the process of extracting larger meaning from data to support evaluation and decision making at various levels within the company. Such analysis may entail using data to reveal information—such as trends, projections, and cause and effect—that might not be evident without analysis. Facts, data, and analysis support a variety of company purposes, such as planning, reviewing company performance, improving operations, and comparing company quality performance with competitors' or with "best practices" benchmarks.

A major consideration relating to use of data and analysis to improve performance involves the creation and use of performance indicators. Performance indicators are measurable characteristics of products, services, processes, and operations the company uses to evaluate and improve performance and to track progress. The indicators should be selected to best represent the factors that lead to improved customer satisfaction and operational performance. A system of indicators tied to customer and/or company performance requirements represents a clear and objective basis for aligning all activities of the company toward common goals. Through the analysis of data obtained in the tracking processes, the indicators themselves may be evaluated and changed. For example, indicators selected to measure product and service quality may be judged by how well improvement in quality correlates with improvement in customer satisfaction.

Partnership Development

Companies should seek to build internal and external partnerships to better accomplish their overall goals. Internal partnerships might include those that promote labor-management cooperation, such as agreements with unions. Agreements may entail employee development, cross-training, or new work organizations, such as high performance work teams.

Examples of external partnerships include those with customers, suppliers, and education organizations. An increasingly important kind of external partnership is the strategic partnership or alliance. Such partnerships might offer a company entry into new markets or a basis for new products or services.

Partnerships should seek to develop longer-term objectives thereby creating a basis for mutual investments. Partners should address the key requirements for success of the partnership, means of regular communication, approaches to evaluating progress, and means for adapting to changing conditions.

Corporate Responsibility and Citizenship

A company's quality system objectives should address corporate responsibility and citizenship. Corporate responsibility refers to basic expectations of the company—business ethics, and protection of public health, public safety, and the environment. Health, safety and environmental considerations need to take into account the company's operations as well as the life cycles of products and services. Companies need to address factors such as waste reduction at its source. Quality planning related to public health, safety, and environment should anticipate adverse impacts that may arise in facilities management, production, distribution, transportation, use and disposal of products. Plans should seek avenues to avoid problems, to provide forthright company response if problems occur, and to make available information needed to maintain public awareness, safety, trust and confidence. Inclusion of public responsibility areas within a quality system means not only meeting all local, state, and federal legal and regulatory requirements, but also treating these and related requirements as areas for continuous improvement beyond mere compliance.

Corporate citizenship refers to leadership and support—within reasonable limits of a company's resources—of publicly important purposes, including the above-mentioned areas of corporate responsibility. Such purposes might include education, resource conservation, community services, improving industry and business practices, and sharing of nonproprietary quality-related information.

▼ INCORPORATING THE CORE VALUES IN THE BALDRIGE AWARD

The ten core values and concepts in the seven award categories are listed next. The Baldrige Award offers a maximum score of 1,000 points:

1. Leadership

2. Information and Analysis

3. Strategic Quality Planning

4. Human Resource Development and Management

5. Management of Process Quality

6. Quality and Operational Results

7. Customer Focus and Satisfaction

▼ BALDRIGE AWARD CRITERIA FRAMEWORK

The framework of the Baldrige award has four basic elements:

1. *Driver.* Senior executive leadership creates the values, goals, and systems and guides the sustained pursuit of customer value and company performance improvement.

2. *System.* System comprises the set of well-defined and well-designed processes for meeting the company's customer quality and performance requirements.

3. *Measures of Progress.* Measures of progress provide a results-oriented basis for channeling actions to delivering ever-improving customer value and company performance.

4. *Goal.* The basic aim of the quality process is the delivery of ever-improving value to your customers.

To receive more information on and an application for the Malcolm Baldrige National Quality Award, contact:

United States Department of Commerce
Technology Administration
National Institute of Standards and Technology
Administration Building, Room A537
Route 270 and Quince Orchard Road
Gaithersburg, MD 20899
(301) 975-2000

You may also write ASQC, which administers the program for NIST:

American Society for Quality Control
P.O. Box 3005
Milwaukee, WI 53201-3005

BALDRIGE AWARD CRITERIA FRAMEWORK
Dynamic Relationships

Goal
- Customer Satisfaction
- Customer Satisfaction Relative to Competitors
- Market Share

Measures of Progress
- Product & Service Quality
- Internal Quality & Productivity
- Supplier Quality

Customer Focus and Satisfaction 7.0

Quality and Operational Results 6.0

System

Management of Process Quality 5.0

Human Resource Development and Management 4.0

Strategic Quality Planning 3.0

Information and Analysis 2.0

"Driver"

Senior Executive Leadership 1.0

256

APPENDIX TWO

Mission and Vision Statements

▼ NAVAL AMPHIBIOUS BASE, CORONADO, CA

Mission Statement
Our mission is to provide administrative and logistic support to fleet activities and our tenant commands, most of which are involved in amphibious and special warfare operations.

Vision Statement
Improving quality service through innovation.

Guiding Principles
We are committed to:

- The highest moral and ethical conduct by all.
- Open and effective communication.
- Caring for our people and their families.
- Solutions through teamwork.
- Enhancing the dignity of every individual.
- Protecting our environment.
- Customer service and fiscal responsibility.
- Achieving personal growth.

- First effort, best effort.
- Monitoring the chain of command and respecting tradition.

▼ AT&T UNIVERSAL CARD SERVICES CORP.

Mission Statement

We intend to be the primary and most-helpful provider of our customers' transactions, payment and selected services needs . . . and to maximize the use of AT&T communications devices and networks.

▼ AT&T TRANSMISSION SYSTEMS

Vision Statement

- Being the best at everything we do, exceeding our customer expectations
- Growing our business to increase in value to customers, employees, shareholders, and communities in which we work
- Remaining integral with Network Systems in the achievement of AT&T's mission

▼ UARCO

Vision Statement

"Our vision is to be the best in all we do as judged by our customers, employees, and suppliers and to be the envy of our competitors."

BIBLIOGRAPHY

Albrecht, Karl, *Service Within*. Homewood, IL: Dow Jones-Irwin, 1990.

Amsden, Davida M., Howard E. Butler, and Robert T. Amsden, *SPC Simplified for Services*. White Plains, NY: Quality Resources, 1991.

Barker, Joel Arthur, *The Future Edge*. New York: William A. Morrow, 1992.

Brown, Mark Graham, *Baldrige Award Winning Quality, How to Interpret the Malcolm Baldrige Award Criteria*. White Plains, NY: Quality Resources, 1991.

Burley-Allen, Madelyn, *Listening: The Forgotten Skill*. New York: John Wiley & Sons, 1982.

Camp, Robert C., *Benchmarking: The Search for Industry Best Practices That Lead to Superior Performance*. White Plains, NY: Quality Resources, 1989.

Carlzon, Jan, *Moments of Truth*. Cambridge, MA: Ballinger, 1987.

Covey, Stephen R., *The 7 Habits of Highly Effective People: Powerful Lessons in Personal Change*. New York: A Fireside Book, Simon & Schuster, 1989.

Crosby, Philip B., *Quality Is Free*. Bergenfield, NJ: New American Library, 1979.

Davidow, William, and Bro Uttal, *Total Customer Service*. New York: Harper & Row, 1989.

Day, George S., *Market Driven Strategy: Processes for Creating Value*. New York: The Free Press, 1990.

Dobyns, Lloyd, and Clare Crawford-Mason, *Quality or Else: The Revolution in World Business*. Boston: Houghton Mifflin, 1991.

Drucker, Peter F., *Managing the Future: The 1990s and Beyond*. New York: Truman Talley Books/Dutton, 1992.

Galvin, Robert W., *The Idea of Ideas*. Schaumburg, IL: Motorola University Press, 1991.

Hanan, Mack, and Peter Karp, *Customer Satisfaction: How to Maximize, Measure, and Market Your Company's Ultimate Product*. New York: American Management Association/AMACOM, 1991.

Harrington, H. James, *Business Process Improvement*. New York: McGraw-Hill, 1991.

Hax, Arnoldo C., and Nicolas S. Majluf, *Strategic Management*. Englewood Cliffs, NJ: Prentice Hall, 1984.

Hinton, Thomas D., *The Spirit of Service*. Dubuque, IA: Kendall Hunt, 1991.

Imai, Masaaki, *Kaizen: The Keys to Japan's Competitive Success*. Kaizen Institute, Ltd. New York: Random House, 1989.

Kawasaki, Guy, *The Macintosh Way*. Glenview, IL: Scott, Foresman, 1990.

Lax, Eric, *Woody Allen*. New York: Alfred A. Knopf, 1991.

Levitt, Theodore, *The Marketing Imagination*. New York: The Free Press, 1986.

Michalak, Donald, and Edwin Yager, *Making the Training Process Work*. New York: Harper Collins, 1979.

————, *The Memory Jogger, A Pocket Guide of Tools for Continuous Improvement*, Methuen, MA: Goal/QPC, 1992.

Nelson, Bob, "Change Comes to the BBC," *Forum Issues*, Vol. 13, Fall 1991.

Petersen, Donald E., and John Hillkirk, *A Better Idea: Redefining the Way Americans Work*. Boston: Houghton Mifflin, 1991.

Quinn, James B., *Intelligent Enterprise*. New York: Free Press, 1992.

Raffio, Thomas, *Quality and Delta Dental Plan of Massachusetts*. Sloan Management Review, Fall 1992.

Reichheld, Frederick F., and W. Earl Sasser, "Zero Defections, Quality Comes to Services," *Harvard Business Review*, September-October 1990.

Senge, Peter M. *The Fifth Discipline: The Art and Practice of the Learning Organization*. New York: Doubleday Currency, 1990.

Sewell, Carl, and Paul B. Brown, *Customers for Life: How to Turn That One-Time Buyer into a Lifetime Customer.* New York: Doubleday Company, 1990.

Walton, Mary, *The Deming Management Method.* New York: Perigee Books/G. P. Putnam, 1986.

Whiteley, Richard C., *The Customer Driven Company: Moving from Talk to Action.* Reading, MA: Addison-Wesley, 1991.

Index